TRANSSEXUALS

TRANSSEXUALS

Candid Answers to Private Questions

by Gerald Ramsey, Ph.D.

The Crossing Press • Freedom, CA 95019

Special thanks to my wife Sherry, for suggesting this project; to John Gill for taking my phone call and giving an unknown writer a hearing; to Ron Stringer for walking me through my first edit; and to Elaine Gill and the staff of Crossing Press for providing a forum.

I also wish to express my gratitude to the American Psychiatric Association and the Harry Benjamin International Gender Dysphoria Association, Inc. for allowing me to reprint relevant diagnostic and clinical standards.

Library of Congress Cataloging-in-Publication Data

Ramsey, Gerald.
   Trannsexuals : candid answers to private questions / by Gerald Ramsey.
         p. cm.
   Includes bibliographical references.
   ISBN 0-89594-790-0
   1. Transsexualism–Miscellanea. 2.Transsexuals–Psychology–
HQ77.9.R36 1996
305.3–dc20
                              95-26804
                              CIP

This book is dedicated to transsexuals,
to the caring professionals who work with them,
and to those with whom they share in the journey of life.

Table of Contents

PART 3: PHILOSOPHICAL, PSYCHOLOGICAL AND SPIRITUAL ISSUES

PART 4: PREPARATIONS

PART 5: NUTS AND BOLTS

APPENDIXES

Foreword

As recently as half a century ago, such as book as Dr. Ramsey's could not have been written. It was not until 1949 that the term "transexual" (spelled with one "s") was coined, by Dr. D. O. Cauldwell. His article appeared in Hugo Gernsback's blue-collar sex-education magazine, *Sexology*, no longer extant and at the time subsidized by Gernsback's popular *Science Fiction* and *Sports Illustrated* magazines. Being sexually explicit, it was banned by the U.S. Postal Inspector, and so had to be sold under the counter from city newsstands. Such was the sexological climate in which transsexualism made its first appearance.

In medicine, the physician who became known as the "father of transsexualism" was Harry Benjamin (1885–1986), formerly a student of Eugen Steinach (1861–1944), the Vienna physician who pioneered experimental antenatal sex reversal in guinea pigs. After World War I, Benjamin settled in New York and become one of the first generation of clinical endocrinologists in America. Instead of retiring in his sixties or seventies, he took up a second career, specializing in transsexualism until he died at the age of 101. His magnum opus, *The Transsexual Phenomenon*, was published in 1966. To avoid charges of obscenity, the publisher omitted all the medical and surgical photographs, which could be obtained only on request from the author. Such was the sexological climate when the term "transsexualism" made its second major medical appearance.

By 1966, the concept of gender had been applied to hermaphroditism by Money (1955) in such expressions as "gender role" and "gender identity" or "gender-identity/role." The concept of gender identity became inseparably linked with transsexualism when, in 1966, the Johns Hopkins Hospital announced the formation of its Gender Identity Clinic and its first sex-reassignment surgery in a case of transsexualism. (This was not, however, the first such case in the United States. There had been an early, short-lived history of transsexual operations by the urological surgeon Elmer Belt in Los Angeles.)

The founding of the Johns Hopkins Gender Identity Clinic gave an impetus for the formation of similar clinics elsewhere.

In 1980, when the American Psychiatric Association published the third edition of its *Diagnostic and Statistical Manual of Mental Disorders, III*, it included a new section on Gender Identity Disorders, under which were subsumed three entities: "Transsexualism," "Gender Identity Disorder of Childhood" and "Atypical Gender Identity Disorder."

Although transsexualism had achieved nosological recognition in the DSM-III, sex reassignment surgery was still the subject of professional dispute, a dispute originating in what may best be called "medical morality," rather than in dispassionate evaluation of outcome data. The medical morality problem has its locus in the mind-body concept, and focused particularly on the issue of intervening surgically and hormonally to change the body to agree with the mind. (Inasmuch as there is no known form of intervention by which to change the transsexual mentality or—more specifically, to change the transsexual gender identity—the alternative is to do nothing.)

For all of its simplicity, the transsexuals' self-description of having a "woman's mind in a man's body" or a "man's mind in a woman's body" accurately locates transsexualism in the brain, which is precisely where it belongs, according to the cumulative evidence of contemporary research. The genetic, gonadal, hormonal and anatomical sex agree with the natal sex of the transsexual, except for the possibility that there is some as yet unidentified anomaly in the sex of the newborn brain. If there is such an anomaly, regardless of whether it is inborn or developmentally later in origin, the questions still requiring an answer are: Where in the brain is it? When did it get there? How did it get there? And how immutably fixated in the brain is it? One hypothesis still awaiting investigation is that of a brain anomaly that alters the sexual body image so as to render it incongruent with the natal sex of the genitalia (Money, 1994). This discrepancy is recognized in the newly voguish term "transgender."

The term "transsexualism," meanwhile, signifies both a diagnosis and, even more importantly, a method of rehabilitation for an otherwise untreatable condition. Sex reassignment is undertaken for the relief of suffering. Although its future history cannot be foretold, it is quite likely that surgery will be eventually superseded by effective methods of prevention, and by effective methods of defixating the transsexual fixation. In the meantime, Dr. Ramsey's book provides a very important source of rehabilitative information for transsexuals and for those with whom they live, work and socialize.

—John Money, Ph.D., Professor of Medical Psychology and Pediatrics Emeritus, Johns Hopkins University and Hospital

Introduction

Imagine ... you wake up in the morning. Your legs are not quite long enough to touch the hardwood floors in your bedroom. Rubbing the sleep from your eyes, you walk to the bathroom and step up onto the small stool, raising your field of vision to include the rectangular mirror. Your insides cry out as you confront a girl with medium-length hair, instead of the short-haired boy who lives in your dreams. You continue to fuss inwardly as you sink back onto the toilet seat. You do stand occasionally to urinate, but it's awkward, and you are fearful your mother will walk in on you again.

Today is Sunday, and you will be expected to dress for church. It is the only day of the week you are required to wear a girl's dress. You survey your closet, moving from one sad selection to the next. Before you know it, you are crying again. Mother will be up soon and the argument will begin. You will say you have nothing to wear, and she will say you have beautiful clothes. "They *are* beautiful dresses," you tell yourself, "but not when I wear them." You can't wait until you are old enough to skip church.

It's not that you dislike church. It's that you can't stand the My-don't-you-look-pretty's and the Girl-you're-going-to-break-many-a-boy's-heart's. They don't mean any harm, but their words seem calculated to slice-and-dice your already faltering self-esteem. You are angry and frustrated as it is, but your despondency is fueled on a regular basis by everyone, your parents, the mailman, your teachers—everyone. No one knows who you are. No one speaks to who you are. No one touches, holds or kisses you for who you are.

Your only refuge is your dreams and waking fantasies, and they are beginning to frustrate you as well. Your favorite fantasies include hunting with your father, playing varsity baseball, having a dirt-clod fight with the other boys (and winning, and going home with the smell of dirt on your clothes), and being a trial lawyer (and after every case the judge will declare, "Young man, you're as good a lawyer as anyone who's stood before this bench").

Next to your weekly pilgrimage to Sunday school, it's the holidays that are the toughest to survive. Christmas is always the same: the family sitting around the tree as they take turns opening presents, saying how "great" the gift is, how it's "just what I wanted." Except the BB gun you want is always a doll, the camping equipment a hope chest, and each pair of jeans comes with a companion frilly top. Once, before grandma died, she gave you a pink party dress with a short note: "Make grandma proud and wear this when you come to visit me. You're too pretty to be a tomboy." This Christmas you will wake up and go downstairs to face more disappointments, continuing proof that no one in your family recognizes you. It's not that they don't love you. It's not that you're invisible—being invisible would be a welcome change. It's that they treat you like a girl.

Now you're twelve, and not long ago you became hysterical, then very ashamed, when you began to menstruate. You had heard about periods, and you had prayed to God that you would never suffer such a fate. You promised God that you'd always be good if you could just not start your period. Every month since then, you've been confronted with "the curse." As if that were not bad enough, your chest is budding; in fact, you are attracting more attention than most, for you have been "blessed" with abundant breasts. Now, when you play football, the guys find excuses to bump into you and grab you.... .

It isn't that you don't like the attention, it's just the wrong kind of attention. It was bad enough that your own body betrayed you, smearing your gender in your face. Now everyone knows that you are becoming a woman. They stare and gape, and the sad part is, they're not really looking at you.

Deep inside the sanctuary of your mind you do, of course, think about romance and sex. But how to make it happen? You imagine being a man and making love to your friend Cindy. You're amazed by your own thoughts. Then a dark cloud drops over the scene. It all seems so improbable. You cry, and you are angry at yourself for crying. You are angry at your parents. You are angry at the world. You are angry at God.

In junior high school, you hear—actually, you read about—transsexuals for the first time. You feel excited at the prospect that you are not alone. You resolve to write a paper on transsexuality for an advanced study class. Although it turns out to be a great paper, you decide not to hand it in. Cindy saw the magazine articles on transsexuals and called them "weird," "gay blades." You don't want anyone to look too closely and think that about you. Again, you're angry at yourself. It's tough enough when others betray you; it's even worse when you do it to yourself.

By the time you enter college, you've figured out you are not a homosexual. You've begun trying to educate your friends and lovers. Some of them understand. Others pretend to understand.

As for you, you just want to be whole—and sooner, not later. So, after years of therapy, cross-dressing and hormones, you have finally scrimped and saved and garnered enough money—together with the inheritance from your grandparents—to pay for the hospital and the surgery. (As you mature as a person and a transsexual, you encounter a new frustration: your health plan will not pay for your gender-reassignment surgery on the grounds that the surgical techniques are "experimental.") You make the last $20,000 deposit on your new life… .

Following your last post-surgical office visit, you assure the doctors and the counselors you'll stay in contact. But you won't. Instead, you'll disappear into your new world, part of the humming current of mankind. You do not wish to stand out. You do not wish to proclaim your new identity, except to the few who held your hand through this, your second birth. Instead you fade into time, walking the road, surmounting the obstacles, singing the song of man.

HAVE YOU MET MS. JONES?

In 1976, as the student member of the gender identity (GID) committee of the Eastern Virginia Medical School in Norfolk, I was asked to evaluate transsexual candidates for the program and to provide therapy for one or two cases—all under close supervision, of course. Naively, and with an arrogance I would learn was typical of inexperienced medical interns, I accepted the challenge. Having "mastered" the more general areas of my chosen profession, I felt that it was time to move on to more exotic experiences.

I thought I had a pretty good idea of what I was getting into. I assumed that transsexuals were "sick" people, effeminate homosexuals who'd fixated on a questionable (if dramatic) way out of the closet, or outright psychotics. I was prepared to find such people unlikeable, undereducated and, on the whole, odd. I was confident that all most of them needed was an accomplished therapist like myself. A little advice and a little male role modeling would turn them around inside a month.

When the phone in my office beeped to announce the arrival of my first transsexual patient, I picked up the chart and walked into the waiting room. The paperwork indicated that S.P. Jones was a preoperative male-to-female transsexual. Accordingly, I looked around the room for a man. Finding only seven or eight adult females, along with several children, I returned to my office puzzled and called my secretary.

"Sarah, where is Mr. Jones?"

"Ms. Jones is in the waiting room," she replied with emphasis. "She's wearing a white dress. And she prefers to be called Sandra."

"A dress!" I thought, my homophobic reaction growing by the moment. "Great!"

I returned to the waiting room and was able to spot only two women in white dresses, one of them a gorgeous blonde. Moving instinctively towards the less striking of the pair, and bracing myself for the worst sort of encounter, I extended my hand and said, "Ms. Jones, please come with me."

When the woman indicated she wasn't Ms. Jones, I realized I'd screwed up again. I turned to the other woman—long, luxuriant hair, delicate, carefully manicured hands, tasteful make-up, a winning smile and a feminine figure to match—and made the best I could of the introduction. As I led the way back to my office, my head was spinning. Was this a joke? Had one or more of my colleagues set me up?

"This is no transsexual," I decided. "This is a woman." It turns out I was wrong in the first place and correct in the second. Sandra was in fact a transsexual, and in nearly all respects a woman.

I pictured what it would have been like if I had met this person under other circumstances. I would never have known that "she" was really a man. I no doubt would have followed all the gender-correct behavior, circa 1976—opening the doors, buying the drinks, et cetera. I realized that if one were to kiss "Ms. Jones," one would never know that he was—technically, at any rate—a man.

Then I caught myself. "If *we* had kissed, I would never have known that he was a man." (This is known in therapeutic jargon as "owning your own thoughts." When a therapist feels intensely about a patient, positively or negatively, he does his best to evaluate the "transference" in terms of the effect of his feelings on his assessment or treatment of the patient. In this way, the therapist minimizes the extent to which he may have mixed his own feelings up with those of the patient.)

As the interview progressed, my thoughts and emotions grew more and more confused. It became clear that while I didn't know who my patient was—or, for the moment, who I was—she did know. It was all I could do to maintain my professional demeanor. During those moments there was only one lost soul in my office, and it wasn't S.P. Jones.

Not that I had any problem asking the routine clinical questions, even those involving sex. It was not the technical aspect of the interview that was causing me havoc, but the emotional aspect, the "heart" part. And although I may not have known who Ms. Jones was, I did know who she *wasn't*. She wasn't a homosexual, she wasn't a drag queen, she wasn't a freak, and she wasn't crazy.

It would be a long time before I gained a sense of the real Ms. Jones. I was a Virginia-born, white, Anglo-Saxon, Protestant, married male. I had attended private schools, traveled a little, and was completing my third university degree. I felt thoroughly "enlightened," if inadequately prepared for what the minds of men and women might present to me as a therapist.

***

I remember one supervisory session with Dr. William Scarpetti and other members of my GID committee, shortly following the interview with Ms. Jones. Although I did not disclose the discomfort I had experienced with my first transsexual patient, they were a seasoned enough group to pick up on it. They focused, most gently, on getting me in touch with the part of myself that had been the most upset about what I had seen and felt. I recall one committee member describing how people often feel when they first meet a transsexual, especially a postoperative transsexual who is comfortable with himself and the choice he has made—how this can challenge one's own sense of gender security, leading to intense discomfort and even, in some cases, to hostility.

It has been eighteen years since I first met Sandra P. Jones. I have since had the opportunity—and, in most cases, the pleasure—of evaluating approximately 500 transsexuals, and personally conducting therapy sessions with more than 100 of them, sometimes in conjunction with their friends and family. I find that the more I learn about transsexuals, the more I learn about myself and the society in which I live.

Over the years, friends and colleagues have suggested I write a book about this work. Although intrigued by the idea, I quickly eliminated the idea of taking a technical approach. I wanted instead to share the heart and soul of what I'd experienced. Just such a volume would have greatly helped me in my early years of working with transsexuals. Acquaintance with the facts—as well as the various myths—about transsexuality would have enabled me to deal more effectively with my own insecurities, thus smoothing the way for the first round of transsexuals who came to me for counsel or evaluation.

This book is an attempt, then, to provide accurate, straightforward information about transsexuality. It is my intention—by presenting the statements, stories, questions and answers that so many have shared with me over the past two decades—to provide knowledge and encouragement, and to help bridge the gaps in understanding that exist between transsexuals, their friends, their families, and others concerned for their health and happiness.

The parts which follow are an attempt to provide a series of snapshots into the evolving world and life of the transsexual. The book is a compilation of hundreds of questions, stories, discussions, statements and answers shared by and with transsexuals and others over the course of the past two decades.

In order to protect the confidentiality of my patients, I have in no instance used a completely accurate history or story of any single person. I have instead mixed aspects of many different patients which, when combined, provide what I believe to be a representative picture of those with whom I have worked. On the other hand, any transsexual, whether a patient of mine or not, should be able to find him- or herself living between these covers.

PART 1:
BOUNDARIES, DEFINITIONS, STEREOTYPES

What is gender dysphoria? What is a transsexual?

In the simplest terms, gender dysphoria is a feeling of being unhappy or depressed about one's own gender. The American Psychiatric Association *Diagnostic and Statistical Manual, IV,* (1994) presents several components of what it calls "gender identity disorder":

a. "a strong and persistent cross-gender identification, which is the desire to be, or the insistence that one is, of the other sex...";

b. "not merely...a desire for any perceived cultural advantages of being the other sex [but] evidence of a persistent discomfort about one's assigned sex, or a sense of inappropriateness in the gender role of that sex";

c. non-concurrent diagnosis of "physical intersex condition," e.g., androgen insensitivity syndrome, also known as congenital adrenal hyperplasia, which occurs when intrabdominal gonads in the form of testes secrete both androgens and estrogens, creating a genetic male with external female genitalia, breasts and vagina, but no cervix;

d. presence of "clinically significant distress or impairment in social, occupational, or other important areas of functioning."

These diagnostic criteria, while providing a relatively broad definition that includes individuals who were left out under earlier, more rigid criteria, are insufficient in and of themselves to establish a diagnosis of transsexuality. Most persons who experience gender dysphoria are not transsexuals. When I write about transsexuals in this book, I am talking about those individuals with gender identity disorder who:

1. are seeking permanent hormone treatment and/or sexual reassignment surgery;

2. have completed some phases of hormone treatment and/or sexual reassignment surgery, and who are satisfied with the outcome;

3. are desirous of the hormone treatment and/or sexual reassignment surgery, but who—for religious, political, financial or other reasons—cannot actively, fully or publicly participate in this process.

In my experience, transsexuality—unlike simple gender identity disorder—is not a transient phenomenon. It could, rather, be described as "immutable in most instances." (It is also extremely rare for psychosis to present as "apparent transsexuality.") The transsexual process—the journey through therapy, cross-dressing, hormone treatment and surgery—is not a flight of fancy; it is the consistent pursuit of physical, emotional, social, spiritual and sexual wholeness, accomplished at enormous personal cost.

Consider the following case samples:

JOHNNIE

Johnnie is thirteen years old and depressed. He has felt like a girl all his life. As a child he played with dolls and other traditional girl's toys. When playing house, he wanted to be the "mommie." Johnnie became particularly upset when puberty arrived and hair grew around the penis he had never come to accept. He was envious of the girls whose breasts were budding, envious of their brassieres and other accoutrements. He wanted to wear dresses, curl his hair and continue to play house (which he did, secretly and as often as possible).

Although Johnnie fantasized frequently about being a girl, he felt guilty about his fantasies. To please his father, he would try to "be a man," but this never seemed to work.

During high school Johnnie became more depressed and began thinking about killing himself. He planned to dress up in a frilly dress and jump off a high bridge near his home. Since he didn't fit in, why go on living? Everyone would be better off if he just disappeared.

Johnnie suffers from gender dysphoria. Further evaluation may show that he is also a transsexual.

MARIA

Maria had had such high hopes for her marriage with Bill. Over the course of the first six months, however, her fantasy of who Bill was and how she would be treated had been shattered by his brutality.

Bill began slapping her around on their wedding night. Along with the physical violence came the equally damaging mental abuse, ripping and tearing away at the fabric of Maria's self esteem. Bill told her she was a "worthless bitch." If she was fifteen minutes late coming home from work, he would accuse her of "whoring around" with other men.

Bill mentally tortured Maria when he was sober. When he got drunk, he was even worse. Bill came from a long line of alcoholic woman-abusers.

Maria would wish, occasionally, that she were a man. She fantasized that if she were a man she would beat Bill, hurt him, make him cry. She would drive him to his knees. The cost to Bill in pain and humiliation would be substantial.

Finally, following years of abuse, Maria began to accept Bill's litany of accusations. Perhaps, deep down inside, she was a "bad woman." She had been told so many times that she was "scum" that she was beginning to buy into it. If only she'd been born a male, rather than a female. At least then she wouldn't be what and where she was today.

While Maria's case is a sad one, and although she is deeply depressed, she is not suffering from gender dysphoria.

Let's take a closer look at Johnnie and Maria's cases. While the issues of gender clearly trouble their lives, it is Johnnie who has, since childhood, been mentally anguished over not having been born a member of the opposite sex. Marie, on the other hand, was perfectly happy being a genetic female until she married and became the wife of a woman-abuser. It was only then that she began to reject who she was—a woman, a wife and a lover to her husband. Maria fantasized that, by being a man, she would be able to avoid the pain inflicted by her sick husband. This fantasy did not come from any inherent unhappiness with herself or her biological gender; rather, it emanated from her desire to be free of the marriage cage.

Maria's depression will lift when she has once again learned to love and respect herself. This will necessitate terminating her relationship with her husband, or his receiving treatment for his abusive behavior toward women. Thus, Maria's depression is related to her own self-concept and how she allows herself to be treated by others, not to her unhappiness with her birth sex.

Johnnie, on the other hand, cannot be happy as long as he is a man. It doesn't matter how he is treated, or how much he is loved or reviled. It doesn't matter how rich he is, or how famous. Johnnie's unhappiness is not a function of his relationship with any partner; rather, it is a function of how he was born and who he is. Johnnie's biological self and emotional self are incongruent, and until they are brought into balance he will remain gender dysphoric.

One might anticipate that there are levels or degrees of gender dysphoria, and indeed there are. Normally, preoperative transsexuals experience varying levels of depression at different times in their lives. During one period they may feel frustrated, but are able to lessen the depth of their despondency by thrusting themselves into their schoolwork or job. Confronted with rejection by a parent, such mild depression may bloom quickly into major depression and a suicide gesture.

On the other hand, one must not be too quick to perceive a pattern. There are case histories of individuals who are unhappy with their biological gender for short periods or phases of their lives. In contrast, the transsexual has rarely if ever been satisfied with his or her biological gender and the accompanying social roles.

One must also be cautious when it comes to taking the individual behavior, out of the context of the whole individual. One dimension—or even two dimensions—of an individual is not enough to diagnose gender dysphoria correctly. It is the combination of many behaviors, beliefs, feelings and statements that makes up gender dysphoria.

TARA

Consider this seven-year-old's response to the question "What do you want to be when you grow up?"

"I want to be king," she brightly replies, her eyes never wavering as she talks.

"Don't you mean you'd like to be queen?" I further inquire.

"Oh no!" she replies without hesitation. "The king is the boss of the kingdom. I want to be the king."

The conversation clearly shows that Tara is responding to issues of power and control. She is not responding to gender issues as they relate to transsexuality. She is well-grounded in her identity as a young girl. Her self-esteem is strong. She wants to be in a position of authority, and my bet is that one day she will.

This "girl who would be king" does not have gender dysphoria, nor is she a transsexual. While Tara seeks the power and authority of the traditional male, she wishes to be a girl first, with all the perquisites of kingship.

DAVIE

Now consider Davie, a twelve-year-old just entering puberty. He has been referred to my office because his parents found out he has been wearing his sister's and his mother's clothes when they are away from home.

"Do you know why you are here?" I ask.

Davie's eyes are cast down, his foot nervously shaking as he responds to my question.

"I wear girls' clothes," he sheepishly responds.

"Why do you wear girls' clothes?" I query.

"It makes me feel good," he replies, his eyes finally meeting mine. "I like how it makes me feel."

"What do you mean?"

"All silky smooth, and I like the smell."

I press further. "What do you do when you are dressed up?"

"I just dress up, that's all." His eyes dip again.

"Are you sure that's all, Davie?" I ask.

Following a long pause, "Well, I whack it...you know, whack it."

Davie is talking about masturbation. Further evaluation discovers that it's been more than a year since he started dressing up in girl's clothes. He especially likes pantyhose, which hold his genitals close to his body. He likes the sensation of the material next to his skin. He likes rubbing himself. The smells of perfume excite him. This behavior began about the time he entered puberty.

"Heck no, I don't want to be a girl," he responds quickfire to my suggestion. "I just like the feeling. I think about..." and he goes on to describe an adolescent fantasy of being with a woman sexually.

Davie likes to wear women's clothes. It sexually excites him to dress in female garments, especially with stockings. If this evolving fetish continues, Davie may well become a transvestite, but he does not have gender dysphoria, and he is not a transsexual.

SUSAN

Susan is fifteen years old. Her friends call her "Sam." She is tall, thin, wears her hair cut short and dresses androgynously. Although she has large breasts for her body frame, few people know it, because she binds them tightly to her chest with a silk wrap-around. This binding, although uncomfortable, does effectively hide her breasts.

Sam has never had a boyfriend. She has never been physically or mentally abused by a male. However, the thought of kissing or being physically intimate with a male makes her feel ill.

She does have a girlfriend, whom she cares about deeply, and with whom she has a sexual and emotional relationship. Sam is the only active love-maker in the couple. She does not allow her girlfriend to kiss or fondle her.

In Sam's dreams and fantasies, she sees herself as a man. When she is sexual with her lover, she imagines herself as having a penis. When she is not pretending to be a man, she is depressed and angry.

Sam does appear to have gender dysphoria. Further evaluation is necessary to determine whether Sam is a transsexual.

TAMMY

A 26-year-old female who lives with her 22-year-old girlfriend Joan, Tammy has had a difficult time accepting her own sexuality. She enters therapy believing she is a transsexual. Perhaps because Tammy's parents have shown disapproval of her lesbian lifestyle, Tammy herself is unhappy with her role in a homosexual relationship.

After a few months of therapy, Tammy comes to realize that being a woman is not at the core of her depression; rather, it is her discomfort with the masculine aspects of herself. She enjoys both pleasuring her partner sexually and receiving a variety of sexual attentions in return. Once she has accepted who she is, including both the feminine and the masculine aspects of her personality, she concludes that although she has suffered from gender dysphoria for more than a decade, she is a lesbian woman, not a transsexual.

The *Merck Manual of Diagnosis and Therapy* (1992) refers to the transsexual's internal feelings as the "private experience of gender role" and to gender role as "the public expression of gender." As displayed by the preceding case histories, the private experience and the public expression of gender are often at variance, especially in the younger transsexual. It is the congruence of private experience and its public expression that he or she so vigorously pursues.

What is the difference between a transsexual and a transvestite?

The *Diagnostic and Statistical Manual, IV,* states the following regarding the person it labels the "transvestic fetishist": "While cross-dressed, he usually masturbates, imagining himself to be both the male subject and the female object of his sexual fantasy." This does not at all describe the typical transsexual, who 1) does not generally obtain sexual pleasure from cross-dressing and 2) does not identify with his or her birth genitals.

Most transsexuals have a history of some heterosexual or homosexual contact. Some have had sexual experiences with both male and female partners. A very small proportion report having had no sexual contacts at all. As a therapist, I look carefully at the quality of the sexual-social contacts to ascertain the level of sexual satisfaction that has been experienced by the individual who is being evaluated. Significant periods of satisfaction in heterosexual, homosexual or bisexual relationships indicate that the individual is probably not a transsexual, even should he or she present with gender dysphoria and/or confusion. If a high level of satisfaction is reported, I would encourage the individual to work on the relationship(s) into which he or she has already entered. For the true transsexual, much more is required.

There are thus several differences between the transsexual who cross-dresses and the transvestite:

1. Transsexual cross-dressing involves the entire spectrum of cross-dressing, from head to toe. Transvestic fetishism at times involves less than complete cross-dressing—focusing, for instance, on underwear or pantyhose.
2. Transsexuals do not generally cross-dress to obtain sexual gratification. Most transsexuals experience a very low libido or sex drive.

3. Transvestites normally spend a significant part of their lives dressed appropriately to their biological birth gender. The mature transsexual does not jump in and out of cross-dressing; his or her cross-dressing is permanent.
4. Transvestites enjoy sexually stimulating themselves, whereas most transsexuals do not touch or even "express ownership" of their birth genitalia or secondary sexual characteristics.

This last point goes directly to one of the distinguishing aspects of transsexuality. The typical preoperative transsexual feels that the genitals attached to his or her body are, in fact, the wrong sexual apparatus. For example, many a preoperative male-to-female transsexual will derisively refer to his sexual organ as "it," "that thing," "the penis," "the body organ," "the mistake" and so forth. Many transsexuals not only use words to disavow ownership, they will not even look at their genitals directly, or in a mirror. Many touch them only to accomplish hygienic functions, and then only with a washcloth.

It is usually even more taboo for a transsexual's bedmate to touch the genitals or, in the case of the biological female, fondle her breasts. When transsexuals do, however infrequently, use their genitals—in intercourse, for example—they most often mentally transform their body image. (For example, if the transsexual is a biological female she may imagine herself as having a penis and penetrating her partner.)

It is of interest to note that many heterosexuals, and some homosexuals, report having experienced the same kind of mental transformation. So while such thoughts may be characteristic of the transsexual, they are not, in themselves, diagnostically determinant.

What is necessary for a diagnosis of transsexuality?

Those who attempt to equate transsexualism and transvestitism are grossly misinformed. I can see how the public might have difficulty with this issue; the professional should not.

Accurate diagnosis of transsexualism requires that a licensed and experienced psychotherapist complete a thorough evaluation, including a complete case history, psychological testing, and an extensive series of interviews or therapy sessions. While any physician can legally make the diagnosis in most states, it is not considered good clinical practice for non-specialists to do so. Those who are not mental-health professionals leave themselves open for ethical and malpractice challenges if they proceed in this delicate treatment field without involving properly trained and experienced mental-health professionals. In most instances, the transsexual diagnosis is made by a panel that includes a clinical psychologist, a psychiatrist and, in some instances, a licensed masters-level therapist, such as a social worker or counselor.

There are several sources of clinical criteria for the diagnosis and treatment of transsexuality. The first is the American Psychiatric Association's *Diagnostic and Statistical Manual, IV* (1994), discussed earlier and excerpted in Appendix A of this volume. The second is the Harry Benjamin Society's *Guidelines for the Treatment of Transsexuals* (1995), which is presented in its entirety at the end of Part V. The third source is the clinical guidelines established by the various gender identity (GID) committees.

The major drawback to using only this manual is its insufficient focus on the consistency of the diagnosis over time. It is day-to-day living as a man or a woman that is the ultimate test of apparent transsexuality. Patients who are reluctant or wishy-washy about their gender decisions should not be recommended for surgery, regardless of any diagnosis of transsexuality.

While I largely concur with the Harry Benjamin International Gender Dysphoria Association, Inc.'s "Standards of Care" (1995), I believe the recommended test periods—the time requirements for cross-living—are too short. (The HBIGDA's "Standards" are reprinted with permission at the end of Part V.)

The most significant difference of opinion among the various gender committees is over the amount of time required before hormonal or surgical interventions should be employed. The time range may vary—from requiring the initial diagnosis only, to as long as a year of cross-dressing before hormonal intervention is approved and commenced. In my opinion, it is seldom if ever prudent to race the transsexual into the operating room or into hormonal therapy. The greater the number and scope of cross-living and therapeutic experiences the transsexual has prior to such major intervention, the better the long-term prognosis.

While the votes have not yet been counted, I project that statistical reports of post-surgical satisfaction will be positively related to the following:

1. proper diagnosis by a licensed mental-health professional;
2. a treatment process guided by an experienced gender team;
3. at least two years of cross-living pre-surgery;
4. at least three years of therapy pre-surgery.

I have no doubt that some will disagree with the need for such lengthy periods of therapy and cross-dressing. I believe, however, that most post-surgical transsexuals, when pressed, will agree that such guidelines, while perhaps uncomfortable, are not harmful to the transsexual and may, in some instances, be crucial to making a proper decision or adjustment.

Even if a person identifies as "transsexual," isn't he or she really homosexual?

We often pretend to understand sexuality when, in fact, we are walking in utter ignorance. The question at the head of this section is a complex one, and must be answered variously.

ANSWER ONE

There is a tendency to assume that when a person is a transsexual, he or she will wind up with a heterosexual orientation after surgery. While this is true in the majority of the cases, it is not universally the case. A transsexual may have a heterosexual orientation, a homosexual orientation, a bisexual orientation—or an asexual orientation. A male-to-female transsexual, for example, may be socially or sexually interested in the opposite sex (in this case, another male), the same sex (a female), both sexes, or neither. (It is important to remember that the mind of the male-to-female transsexual is female.)

ANSWER TWO

The *Diagnostic and Statistical Manual, IV* (1994) states that heterosexual and bisexual men who cross-dress in order to experience sexual excitement should also be diagnosed as having "transvestic fetishism." Many heterosexual, homosexual, bisexual and asexual transsexuals—both male-to-female and female-to-male—regularly cross-dress. Some transsexual individuals are (and others are not) sexually stimulated by cross-dressing.

ANSWER THREE

Just as a heterosexual does not require a partner to be considered heterosexual, the homosexual does not have to have a partner to be considered homosexual. Thus, it is not the presence of a sexual partner that determines our orientation; it is who we are inside. I remind the reader that the average preoperative transsexual is, if anything, "hyposexual" (i.e., has a very low sex drive). An extremely high libido would contraindicate transsexuality in all but the rarest of cases.

ANSWER FOUR

The questioner is often asking about a male-to-male sexual relationship in which one of the partners assumes a more submissive (i.e., traditionally feminine) sexual stance. However, whether a partner is typically a "pitcher" or a "catcher" is not necessarily related to gender. The fact that a male, for example, is a passive partner, does not necessarily mean that he wishes to be a female. He may simply prefer to take a passive stance in some sexual situations.

So, if a man wants to be a woman, is he really a homosexual?

Yes. Perhaps. No. Transsexuality is no more related to homosexuality than it is to IQ, socioeconomic status, religion or race.

What does the term "intersex" mean?

"Intersex," according to *Dorland's Medical Dictionary* (1988), refers to "an individual who shows intermingling, in varying degrees, of the characteristics of each sex, including physical form, reproductive organs, and sexual behavior." By definition, then, an individual who is "intersexed"—a hermaphrodite or pseudohermaphrodite—is not a transsexual. The intersex individual has a biological disorder. It is not psychologically determined, and psychotherapy, while it may be useful, will not under any circumstances lead to a "cure."

The following is a general summary of the characteristics of the hermaphrodite and pseudohermaphrodite.

The Hermaphrodite has at least one morphological contradiction (where the gonadal tissue and the genitalia are incongruent or contradictory, e.g., an individual with a penis who has female gonadal tissue, or an individual with a vagina who has male gonadal tissue; it is also possible to have both male and female genitals and contradictory gonadal tissue); has both male and female gonadal tissue; and rates XX or XY on chromatin test. (The X and Y chromosomes determine the ultimate sex of a person, with the pairing of the female and male gamete determining the sex. The female partner's gamete contributes one X chromosome to the pairing. The male gamete determines the sex by contributing one X chromosome to make XX (a female) or one Y chromosome to make an XY pairing (a male). The male contributes the X and Y on an almost 50:50 basis.)

The male pseudohermaphrodite has at least one morphological contradiction and only male gonadal tissue. He rates XY on the chromatin test. The female has only female gonadal tissue. She rates XX on the chromatin test.

Intersexuality is like transsexuality in that sufferers from both conditions experience gender confusion. They feel alone, out of place, depressed and frustrated. The "Why me, God?" syndrome is common to both cases. In some respects, the intersex individual may experience greater difficulty because he or she is not biologically "whole," as is the transsexual.

Both the transsexual and the intersexed individual are dissatisfied with their biological gender status, experience gender dysphoria, and seek many of the same or similar surgical and hormonal resolutions. And while it is inappropriate to have intersexed patients in a transsexual program, because they experience many of the same psychological problems, they are appropriate candidates for treatment by a GID committee.

Would a legitimate surgery team be likely to operate on any and all persons who meet the diagnostic criteria for transsexuality?

I should hope not! The transsexual diagnosis, while necessary, is only the first step in the process. There are instances in which persons who meet the diagnostic criteria would not be considered for surgery by most teams. While they may be encouraged to seek psychological treatment, no legitimate surgery team would consider sexual-reassignment surgery on:

- **Individuals who are practicing drug addicts or alcoholics**

Many transsexuals have used alcohol and drugs in the attempt to cope with their gender dysphoria and feelings of hopelessness. Most GID teams are more than willing to accept candidates who have received treatment for chemical dependency, who are sober and actively working a twelve-step recovery program. When a practicing alcoholic transsexual does present herself to our team, she does not encounter rejection; rather, we explain that we must first deal with the alcohol problem, and that only then will we focus on transsexuality.

- **Individuals who exhibit serious mental illness or impairment**

I am aware of no GID team that will operate on individuals who cannot give informed consent. This includes people with extremely low IQs, as well as mentally ill individuals. As with substance-abuse, most teams will consider individuals with mental illness, and even those with a history of suicide attempts, if they have received appropriate treatment and exhibited continued improved mental health.

- **Individuals who are legally classified as children in the state in which they live and/or in the state in which they will undergo surgery**

The question of minors is raised more often than one might anticipate. In many cases, the natural father, natural mother, pediatrician and child psychologist support an adolescent's decision to receive sexual reassignment surgery. However, from a legal standpoint, the consent offered by parents or guardians is unlikely to stand up in court. Most informed surgeons will counsel waiting.

- **Individuals who for medical reasons (obesity, advanced age, heavy smoking, etc.) are regarded as poor candidates for surgery**

All transsexuals experience gender dysphoria prior to therapy and surgical reassignment. Surgical intervention should not take place unless there is good reason to believe that the transsexual will be better off emotionally—and that any remaining psychological problems will better lend themselves to resolution—following surgery. Because of the importance of this decision, I believe such determinations are best made by a team of experienced clinicians, physicians and surgeons, and not by solo flyers.

All transsexuals experience some level of clinical depression. Therapy's role in the process is to help transsexuals confront and resolve as many of their other life problems as possible prior to surgery. It is therefore not in the best interests of a diagnosed transsexual to move along too quickly in the process, to rush through the stages or skip stages in the process of acclimating to change. Each stage affords the transsexual opportunities to adjust to the many emotional, physical, spiritual and financial challenges that accompany transformation. It is my belief that if we could magically take the transsexual from A to Z in one giant step, the results in many instances would be disastrous. So, while the transsexual's heart and soul unrelentingly press for rapid change, the transgender team's protocol (see Part V) slows down the process to allow time for adjustment.

Are there more male than female transsexuals?

As recently as ten years ago, nearly all the people presenting themselves to GID committees were male-to-female candidates. The 1994 *Diagnostic and Statistical Manual, IV* states that "data from smaller countries in Europe with access to total population statistics and referrals suggest that roughly one per 30,000 males and one per 100,000 adult females seek sex-reassignment surgery." If accurate, this would mean there are about 4,500 male-to-female transsexuals and 1,350 female-to-male transsexuals in the United States.

To understand this apparent discrepancy, it is important to take a look at the "state of the art" treatment, especially in plastic and micro-vascular areas. While both male-to-female and female-to-male reassignment surgeries are complex, it is much easier, from a technical point of view, to perform castration on the biological male and create a neo-vagina than it is to perform a total hysterectomy on a biological female and create a neo-phallus. To this day, the surgical outcome for the neo-vagina yields superior aesthetic, as well as functional, aspects.

In recent years, as surgical techniques have improved, especially in the field of micro-surgery, the number of female-to-male candidates has rapidly risen. Our clinic's most recent data is 3:2 male-to-female requesting information, but 2:1 female-to-male actually committed to undergoing surgery. These female-to-male candidates have typically already met the therapy and cross-living requirements of the committee. When asked why they did not present to the committee earlier, their reply is nearly always the same: "I had seen pictures of what surgery could offer in the past, and I didn't feel it was worth it. I am here now because advances in technique have led to better appearance, sensation and function."

It is my belief that there are nearly equal numbers of biological males and females who experience the transsexual phenomenon—in other words, that the occurrence of transsexuality directly corresponds to the number of males and females in the general population. I would predict that as surgical outcomes become qualitatively similar for both groups, approximately half of those who complete the process will be biological females.

It makes me angry that gender problems are called "disorders." How do you feel about such diagnoses?

First, you should be glad there *are* diagnoses that involve gender disorders. Without such categories, transsexuals would be subjected to inaccurate diagnoses and descriptions, ranging from "schizophrenic," "delusional" and "dissociative" to "transvestitism" and other paraphilias (fetishes).

Secondly, and tough as this may sound, transsexuals are *not* normal. To say that a transsexual—or someone who has a cleft palate or a congenital heart defect—is entirely without anomaly is truly delusional. To say that all of these patients can be rendered near-normal with the help of modern psychology and medicine is accurate.

So be glad there are diagnostic categories (even if they are imperfect) relating to gender issues and to surgical/psychological techniques that help transsexuals attain wholeness. For while transsexuals may feel "normal" inside as regards their gender identity, they will not be truly whole until inside and outside match up.

Again, to state that the transsexual does not deviate from the biological and psychological norm is to kid oneself. In my judgment, it is best to consider the real problems inherent in this disorder and resolve them, not deny them. I see no benefit in taking an ostrich approach to physical and psychological well-being.

Is transsexuality strictly a Western phenomenon?

I have come to believe in the universality of the transsexual phenomenon.

It is accurate to state that much of the original surgical research and experimentation took place in the West. Many of the genital-reconstruction techniques were developed initially for burn and trauma patients whose genitalia and other external features had been damaged or destroyed. As psychology and medicine learned more about the transsexual and his unusual requirements, it was but a few steps from cosmetic surgery for burn patients to sexual-reassignment surgery. To the extent, then, that psychotherapy and medicine first recognized and worked with transsexuality as a clinical problem, it is Western in flavor.

The longer I am in practice, however, the more aware I become of the apparent global nature of this phenomenon. I have worked with transsexuals from across the United States, from Canada, Mexico, South America, Poland, the Netherlands, Europe, Asia and Africa, with the very rich, the middle class and the poor. I have seen patients from big cities, small towns and tiny villages. They come to me, interpreter in tow, from areas with few newspapers or televisions. Several of them have been surprised to find out that they are not alone, that thousands of others all over the world share their condition and their hope.

In short, the phenomenon seems to cut across culture, race, income level and geographic region.

PART 2:
FAMILY, FRIENDS, LOVERS

I think you are an evil S.O.B. If it wasn't for doctors like you, my baby wouldn't be getting butchered up. How can you live with yourself?

As you might expect, it is not unusual for the professionals who work on GID committees to bear the brunt of hostile accusations from parents or friends, who, for the most part, have little or no understanding of the transsexual phenomenon. Some of these well-meaning if misinformed people seem to believe that if the committees closed, no one would seek out a surgeon, that all who suffer from gender dysphoria and other transgender problems would miraculously come to accept themselves and live happily ever after.

Historically speaking, much of the early genital reconstruction developed as a response to tragic burn and accident cases in which exposed body parts and organs—ears, eyelids, genitalia—had been burned off or otherwise destroyed. Most of the techniques used in sexual-reassignment surgery originated in such situations. Their use in transsexuality was an afterthought, albeit a creative one.

Genital reconstruction is now performed in a number of countries, including Belgium, Canada, the Netherlands, England, Sweden, Mexico, Taiwan, the Caribbean nations and the United States. For anyone with the money, there are plenty of doctors willing to perform the surgery.

Committees such as the one in which I participate are the preoperative transsexual candidate's best hope of realizing a legitimate assessment of his or her chances for a positive outcome. The majority of the transsexuals with whom I have worked have been in the process of "becoming" for a decade or more. This process may include the years between making a decision and reaching majority, the years in therapy while cross-dressing and cross-living, in addition to time spent in hormonal therapy, electrolysis and elective surgery.

No legitimate surgery team or committee, in my opinion, would consider operating on a candidate who had not gone through extensive counseling, medical screening and cross-living. Operating on a unscreened or underassessed individual would place the physician at medical malpractice risk and the patient in harm's way.

So, by way of answering this apparently hostile question, I would first encourage the questioner to express his or her anger and fears—as a way to get past rage or uninformed objections and into professional counseling. I have seen many parents, friends and mates arrive at a place where they are able to *listen*, thereby gaining a broader perspective on what legitimate therapy and, in some cases, surgery has to offer. It is most important to get accurate, unbiased information into the hands of the parents, mates and friends of the transsexual.

Of those who present themselves to my committee as candidates for surgery, only a fraction follow through. With therapy, many find they are not really transsexuals, but suffer instead from some other condition related to gender dysphoria. If legitimate doctors, clinics and committees were not available to those who experience gender dysphoria, the number of inappropriate surgeries and unsatisfactory outcomes would doubtless rise.

To date, no postoperative transsexual with whom I have worked has later decided it was a mistake. I am aware, however, of others who have been unhappy with their decision. In each instance, the patient elected to take the fast train to sex-reassignment surgery. I urge those transsexuals who read this book to consider taking the "local" instead of racing for third-class seats on the "express."

It's easy for you doctors to pontificate, but how would you feel if your own child were a transsexual?

After nearly two decades of experience as a professional psychologist, I do not believe that transsexuals, heterosexuals or homosexuals choose their orientation. While there are many things you can do to help or hinder your child, the one thing you cannot create or un-create is a transsexual.

If I had the choice, I would not want my own or anyone else's child to be a transsexual. Transsexuals have an arduous road to travel. They must go through psychological, emotional and social turmoil, not to mention physical pain and economic sacrifice.

More broadly, I would not wish my children to have any birth defect that would make their lives more difficult.

If one of my children were, however, to turn out a transsexual—or experience gender dysphoria, or have any other similar problem—I would hope that I would take the time to listen, learn and accept. While I would be sad that my child had to go through the many emotional hoops and physical challenges required, I would love my child and support him or her.

Being a human being, I might, like many others, be tempted to "bargain with God," or attempt to deny that the problem exists, or blame someone, or cover over my worries with alcohol or drugs, before finally coming to grips with my own fears and reestablishing support for my son or daughter.

The journey is not an easy one, and my child would be no exception. Just because I intellectually know what to do does not mean that I would not have difficulty. I would no doubt talk with a psychologist myself.

My son is decorated Marine, the father of three healthy children and a Christian. How can he possibly be a "she"?

This question focuses on the packaging. What we see or wish to see in someone we love is not necessarily what is actually there. Many young transsexuals throw themselves into their careers, immersing themselves for a period of time in so much work and responsibility that the wounds to their personality are not apparent. Some transsexuals attempt to identify with careers that are antithetical to transgender issues. These are transsexual candidates who are in the military, transsexuals who have children and who have strong religious backgrounds.

The real question is, how was this young man able to survive so long as a man? How was he able to successfully live out so many roles that were incongruent with his internal template?

It was only when his children were all grown up and he was eligible for retirement that he felt he could finally seek help. To have done so earlier would have surely led to his discharge from the Marines. After a period of therapy he progressed into cross-dressing quickly, making up for lost time during his "first life."

Around twenty percent of the transsexuals with whom I worked have been married, and about fifty percent were married and had children. The majority of these transsexuals married young—as a means, in part, of dealing with their gender dysphoria. They typically hoped that by marrying and having children they would grow to accept their biological gender. (For many, it did temporarily salve the hurt and confusion.) Some female-to-males hoped that the process of giving birth might somehow change their minds, leading to an acceptance of their birth gender.

Jeannie provides a good example. She felt that if she had a child, it would somehow establish—or force her to accept—her female identity. ("After all, only a female can have a baby.") Jeannie put her mind and body to the task, giving birth to not one but three children. She focused her energy on being a good mother. It wasn't until she was forty-four—and her youngest child had turned eighteen—that she felt free to take steps toward undergoing reassignment surgery. When Jeannie finally made up her mind and announced her decision, family, friends and church descended on her en masse to "bring her to her senses." She had played her role well.

John's case provides an interesting contrast. Like Jeannie, he married to mask and overwhelm his underlying self, siring four children in stair-step fashion. It did not take long for his depression to sink to unbearable levels. When he shared his feelings with his wife, they went into counseling for over a year. They finally agreed to stay married until the children were older. While they lived together, John continued therapy and explored his feminine side by cross-dressing in private and on special trips away from the house. For a time, his wife hoped that he would change his mind. It eventually became apparent that the marriage was not going to work. When John's youngest child turned thirteen, his wife decided she could not carry on the charade any longer, and they separated. John became Mary Anne, and the children stayed with their biological mother.

If we could discern the future, we would all no doubt change many things. This is also true for the transsexual. Those who married and had children did so, in most cases, to clarify or rescue an unhappy life, not to complicate it further. The suppression of the emotional and spiritual self, which many transsexuals attempt, is almost always unsuccessful.

Getting back to the original question: "How can he possibly be a 'she'?" Your son was born with a rare anomaly—transsexuality—and your acceptance of this condition hinges on your understanding the following:

Your son had no choice in the matter. The fact that he labored as long and as hard as he did in his role as a man is remarkable.

Transsexuality appears to be immutable; that is, there are few if any known instances of properly diagnosed adult transsexuals changing their minds and accepting their birth bodies.

The real question should have been "Why was he not born a 'she'?" Or better, "Why was she not born a 'she'?"

What did I do to make my child a transsexual?

America has been eating guilt for breakfast since the Jamestown settlers first landed in Virginia. Jane is born prematurely. "Was it my diet?" Jimmy has a learning disability. "It runs in your family, dear." Bob married outside the family religion. "We didn't spend enough time on religious training." Julie is pregnant. "If you hadn't let her stay out so late, it would never have happened."

Then there is the silently nourished personal guilt. Take the case of Anna, the mother of a transsexual who blamed herself because of one incident in her youth. In college, Anna had a single sexual episode with a girlfriend. Janet's mother had just died, and she was distraught. In her attempts to comfort her friend, one thing lead to another and they ended up having oral-genital sex. Anna felt enormously guilty at the time and later blamed herself when her son expressed his desire to become a girl. She spent many sleepless nights worrying that her one-time episode somehow evidenced a "loose gene," as she called it.

Even though we intellectually realize how illogical such ideas are, we are still slaves to our guilty hearts. The parents of the transsexual are no exception to this pitfall. "If Johnny's father had been a better role model..." "If Sandy's mother hadn't slept around so much..." "If grandmother hadn't spoiled Bob..."

I am aware of no incident, no accident, no terrible single trauma that ever "caused" an individual to become a transsexual. While there is no absolute evidence of a biological basis for transsexuality, I can assure you that there is likewise little good evidence supporting the "nurture" argument. As I interview transsexuals, I may hear about incidents of rape, or physical, sexual or emotional abuse, but these situations do not appear to arise any more often in the lives of transsexuals than they do in the lives of other classes of patients. To be sure, transsexuals must deal with the emotional repercussions of such unfortunate occurrences. However, these are unlikely to be the root cause of transsexuality.

In the parents' attempt to understand how this awful thing came to befall their child, they most frequently point the finger at themselves, each other, or at their family trees. It is my experience that such accusations must run their course. Even if family members are in therapy and are continually reassured that it is no one's fault, they appear to need—or perhaps they expect—to go through this phase prior to accepting their child's transsexuality.

In most instances, the parent must go through a period of mourning the loss of their baby girl or boy. It is only afterwards that they are able to accept and welcome into their lives their new son or daughter. Most families do get past their guilt and, ultimately, accept the transsexual. A review of family histories shows that the majority of the parents with whom I have talked remembered minor incidents that made them realize something was "different" about their child. In most cases they did not know what to make of the "difference" until later, when their son or daughter came out as a transsexual. Most parents of transsexuals can, with hindsight, pick out scores of early indicators they have ignored or forgotten. This doesn't mean that earlier intervention would have prevented the development of transsexuality in their child, for there is little evidence that transsexuality can be successfully treated with therapy alone.

Many times the family will go through a period of rejecting the transsexual in the hope that the child will change his or her ways, grow out of it, or fall in love with someone who will "straighten him/her out." After months or several years, most family members come to accept the unalterable reality of their loved one's gender anomaly. It is only when the parents realize that the transsexual is not rejecting them, but rejecting his or her biological birth gender, that family ties begin to reconnect. In fact, when the transsexual is finally approved and loved for the person he or she is, longstanding barriers to interpersonal intimacy quite often fall away.

I have prayed and prayed for my daughter, and she still wants to become a man. What else can I do?

I encourage you to continue to pray for your daughter. Even better, I encourage you to pray *with* your daughter, if your point of religious reference is hers as well. I understand, however, from clerics of various religions that God's answer to prayer may not always be what you want it to be—or the answer may not arrive within your time frame. Many people pray to God, asking the same question over and over, but are unwilling to accept the answer. Instead they repeatedly ask God the same question, hoping for a second opinion that is more in step with their own desires.

There are increasing numbers of clergy who believe that conditions such as homosexuality and transsexuality have a biological basis. If so, they argue, judgments as to right and wrong in such matters are more appropriately left to God and the individual. However, I always recommend that my patients seek counseling from a priest, rabbi or other cleric when they are having spiritual problems. Those who approach this issue with an open heart almost always reach a point of acceptance.

My advice to the mother quoted above is "Love your daughter. Find a member of the clergy you can talk to. Pray together, and see if together you can find the answer. If your daughter will not pray with you, do so alone—but *listen* for the answer. When your daughter reaches her final decision, continue to love her and pray for her. Even as a son, this child is your own."

How does transsexuality most commonly affect families?

Many well-meaning parents have responded to their child's "difference" with strategies to force or coerce the child into normalcy. Biological males are forced to go to military academies, females to all-girl preparatory schools. The belief that the strict regimen and appropriate role models will "whip them into shape" turns out to have been an illusion.

When the child does not respond as hoped, it is not uncommon for mom and dad to project their grief and anger onto one another. Such mutual recriminations often lead to marital conflict and, in some cases, divorce. If there was a homosexual or transvestite relative on either side of the family tree, such information is taken as "proof" that one parent's genetics are at the origin of the problem.

It is not uncommon for children to feel guilty when their parents fight, separate or divorce. In this case the transsexual child will often accept and internalize the guilt, believing that if he or she had been a "good girl" or a "good boy" there would have been no problem, no divorce, that the family would have stayed together.

In some cases, even when parents come to understand intellectually that neither they nor their partners are to blame, they are unable to find their way back to each other. Sometimes, with the flame of their love faltering, they do not have the energy or courage to strive toward reconciliation.

Mothers are generally able to adapt and accept the transsexual child more easily than fathers. This is true regardless of the biological gender of the child. In my experience, mothers are more likely to be the confidantes of both male-to-female and female-to-male transsexuals.

Fathers, while they do tend to reach a level of acceptance, clearly have a more difficult time. As you might anticipate, fathers have particular problems when the transsexual child is a biological male. It is somewhat easier on fathers when there are one or more other biological male sons who accept their own birth gender, and somewhat more difficult if the transsexual male is the only son and child. Some fathers have expressed the belief that their sperm is defective, that they are somehow not men themselves—how could this have happened otherwise? While the typical father is conflicted when his daughter seeks to become a male, ultimate acceptance appears to come more easily in this case.

When it comes to counseling, fathers tend to respond to intellectual, legalistic, scientific arguments. I often begin by discussing how widespread the phenomenon of transsexuality is, how it affects individuals of all races, sexes, religions, cultures and nationalities. Fathers tend to grasp onto the technical and historical elements, enabling them to formulate a pseudo-academic theory of their own.

Mothers, on the other hand, are more often affected by emotional and social variables. It is the pain and suffering, the inconceivable unfairness of this apparent tragedy, that draws the mother to protect and nurture her child, often in a counterproductive fashion.

Over the past eighteen years, of the parents who have accompanied their child on his or her first visit to my office, fully 95 percent have been mothers. It is rare to see a father. This holds true whether the transsexual is a biological male or female. The father is more likely to come later, often after the entire family has pulled together and are in the process of accepting and supporting the transsexual child. The father often comes in order to gain some understanding of and—I state with utmost respect—absolution for what has occurred.

Brothers and sisters of transsexuals also experience guilt, but to a far lesser degree than their parents. While mother and father seldom seriously question their own sexuality and orientation, siblings are frequently confronted with intense concerns and fears. They may begin to wonder what the future holds for them, in terms of sexual identity. Less frequently reported is the sibling's fear that his or her children may turn out transsexual. In my opinion, the inheritability of this very infrequent phenomenon is not something over which family members need worry themselves. There is absolutely no evidence—such as, for example, families with generation after generation of transsexuals—to justify such a concern.

It is during the younger teenage years, 13 to 17, that siblings tend to have the most difficulty. During this time, they are in school and living at home. Even if a teenager accepts his or her transsexual sibling, it is bound to create social stress at school when peers become aware of the situation. Siblings on the whole tend to cope better as young adults, when they are living independently of their parents.

It appears that the more secure family members are with their own sexuality and identity, the better equipped and able they are to empathize and cope with the transsexual. And, as you might expect, the healthier the family, the healthier and better-adapted the transsexual.

When and how should I tell my family I am a transsexual?

The obvious must be stated: you must accept yourself for who you are before you can expect others to accept you. Quite often, transsexual candidates will say that people look at them strangely. After further conversation, I become aware that at least a part of the problem is their own doubts and fears about themselves. If you are comfortable with who you are, so will be the people with whom you come in contact. On the other hand, if you are nervous, uncomfortable or self-hating, these attitudes will be reflected by the people around you.

As for when to tell the family, I advise my transsexual clients to look for a window of opportunity when the family is not in crisis—a day with plenty of time, no schedule to keep and free of stress. ("When" may occur at different times with different family members.) It is not uncommon for a sister or mother to be told first, with the more sympathetic female later breaking the news to the father or brothers. In most cases, there are one or two people in the transsexual's family who are more approachable than the others, and the transsexual's perception of who will and who will not accept him or her is usually accurate.

The most commonly reported responses from such family members include:

"I always knew there was something special about you. Your refusal to play with dolls or wear dresses, your upset stomach each afternoon you had dance lessons! Knowing this answers a lot of questions for me. Now it all makes sense."

"Honey, I've known this all your life. Inside you've always been a girl. It breaks my heart to think about all the pain and loneliness you must have endured."

It is refreshing to report that most families, even the hard-liners, tend to arrive at a level of acceptance after they have gained a better understanding of transgender issues. When describing themselves to their families, the transsexuals with whom I have worked most often begin by recalling their lives growing up—how they felt, how relationships went, and so forth. The story culminates with the sharing of where they are today, and of how much they need their family's love and understanding. (In some families the "secret" was shared in early life with one family member, often a sister.)

In a small number of cases the family is invited to my office, where the transsexual shares with them his or her future plans. This format is used most frequently when it is anticipated that one or two family members will vigorously object.

A very small group of transsexuals see their worst fears real-ized and are, in fact, shunned by or cast out of their biological families. In some of these cases the parents feel that they must choose between their religious faith and their child. Most par-ents and siblings, however, when they realize that their choice is between accepting (on some level) the transsexual relative or losing him, do opt for acceptance.

My daddy is a girl now, clothes and all. Does that mean I'm going to become a girl, too?

I am assuming the transsexual parent is fully committed to the process and therefore certain about his or her decision. If he or she is not absolutely certain, it is inappropriate to present this potentially confusing situation to a child.

Unfortunately, it is often the angry spouse of the transsexual who brings up the topic, out of frustration. It is never helpful for parents to attack or degrade one another. Even if you do not like or approve of your former marriage partner, it will not help your child if you are verbally abusive to the other parent. If you want your child to spend the better part of his or her life in therapy, then continually present your former partner in a bad light.

If the decision is made to explain the situation to a young child, I would suggest answering honestly, in a vocabulary he or she can understand, somewhat as follows:

"Yes, your daddy is becoming a girl. Something was broken when daddy was born, and the doctors are fixing it." In the case of a male father and child, I would then address any self-doubts by saying: "You are a boy and will grow up to be a man. You are not broken, so the doctors will not have to fix you. You are just right the way you are." I would conclude by reminding the child that both parents love him.

Notice that the original question (posed by a seven-year-old boy) focused on the clothing and exterior aspects of gender. This shows the level at which he is thinking, and your answers—and any subsequent discussion—should focus on this level. It would not be particularly helpful to launch into a discourse on brain physiology and gender choice. It is best to give direct, honest, uncomplicated answers.

Given the choice, however, I would not confront children with such information until they are grown up. To understand and accept transsexuality is hard enough for mature adults.

Where young children are involved, I have seen the situation handled in several ways. The most common approach involves the parents continuing to live together until the children are older and thus better able to cope with the father or mother's change of sexual identity.

A second, and in many cases optimal, approach is for the transsexual to take an extended sabbatical from the family, until the children are older and better able to comprehend what is going on. Then, when they are mature, the whole story may be shared and discussed.

A third approach, discussed earlier, is to honestly share the situation with the children, answering their questions in language they can understand. However, to attempt to explain to young children what few adults can understand may not be the most favorable approach.

A fourth approach, where the ex-spouse seeks court protection for the children, legally denying any access or contact with the transsexual spouse, is the least constructive option, insofar as it focuses the child's attention on the fact that something horrible has happened and that the court has forced his or her parent to go away.

During the transsexual parent's period of "becoming," there is an intense focus on self and the many changes to which he or she is adapting. This type of egocentric concentration, while essential for successful movement along the transsexual path, may not lend itself to optimal parenting. (This is, of course, a general statement; there are many transsexuals who have done an excellent job parenting during this phase.)

For children over sixteen years of age who are adapting to adolescence without a lot of problems (e.g., drug abuse, major school conflicts or run-ins with the law), the third approach—by which the children are encouraged to maintain a relationship with their transsexual parent—may be appropriate. If it becomes too difficult for them, they are certainly old enough to say so. While there are potential risks and challenges to children even at this age, the positive connection to the biological parent may outweigh the negatives.

As a therapist, my goal is not to tell transsexuals or their families exactly what to do, but to help them look at the options and make informed decisions. And although the ultimate decision is theirs, not mine, I invariably press the parents to give priority to what will be best for the children.

My daughter is a transsexual. Why is she so obsessed with sex?

"You raise a very interesting subject," I responded. "Why do you say your daughter is obsessed with sex? Does she talk about sex or sexual topics to excess?"

"Well...actually, she rarely talks about 'sex' per se. But isn't sex what transsexuality is all about?"

I went on to explain that most transsexuals have a very low—or in some cases a nonexistent—"sex drive," in terms of both physical interest and response. While transsexuals may express an excessive interest in issues relating to sex roles, or to sexuality in general, they are if anything *undersexed*, in terms of making sexual contacts and of personal physical sexual gratification. The transsexual's gratification is more the result of adequately satisfying his or her sexual partner, and in being able to do so in a chosen gender-specific manner (i.e., as a biological man or woman would).

In fact, a high level of sexual performance, whether with a partner or in masturbation, raises a red flag as to whether the individual is truly a transsexual. While there are no absolutes, gender-dysphoric individuals with extremely high physical sex drives and/or who are extremely active masturbators rarely turn out to be transsexuals. (I have seen a few exceptions.)

One complicating factor that reduces sexual response in the transsexual is the effect of artificial introduction of hormones of the opposite sex. For example, the male-to-female transsexual who is taking a female hormone such as estrogen as part of his treatment is actually suppressing the effect of his body's naturally produced male hormones. This further reduces his libido or sex drive. It is reduced even more when surgical castration occurs and the source of the male hormone testosterone is removed.

In several instances I have had transsexuals report an increase in sexual interest following hormone treatment and/or surgery. When explored in depth, however, the increase in sexual drive turns out to be psychological, not physical, in nature. Transsexuals most often report being excited about the secondary sex characteristics that accompany the hormone treatment, which may serve to improve their self-esteem and, consequently, their willingness to consider participating in sexual situations.

The answer to the following question, often asked of the preoperative female-to-male transsexuals, is quite telling: "If you had to choose between being able to stand and urinate like a biological male, or being able to use your new penis to have sexual intercourse, which would you choose? Remember, assume you can only do one of the two."

It may surprise you to know that nearly 100 percent respond that they would choose standing to urinate, which is male-specific behavior in most cultures, a semi-public behavior that helps define male gender.

For female-to-male transsexuals, one of the most freeing aspects of the gender-reassignment process is mastectomy or breast reduction. Again, think in terms of sex role. The breasts of the preoperative female-to-male transsexual proclaim to the world that she is female, not male. Most of the female-to-male transsexuals with whom I have worked report that their "chest reduction," as they prefer to call it, had a greater impact on their self-esteem and quality of life than did the subsequent construction of the neo-phallus.

In my experience, then, it is the sex role, not any specific sexual activity, that is most urgently sought by the transsexual.

I am in love with a transsexual. After surgery, what the odds we'll stay together?

A significant minority of transsexuals bring their wives, husbands or significant others with them on their first interview with the therapist. A surprising number of these couples plan to stay together after the surgery is completed. While I do not have exact figures, some of these couples actually do stay together. However, most such marriages do not work out.

The second and larger group includes individuals who have fallen in love with the transsexual during his or her transition period. These relationships appear to have a better chance, perhaps because both partners have been working towards acceptance of the transsexual process from the outset.

If you really want to improve the odds of staying together post-surgery, it is important to do what any successful couple learns to do: communicate. You need to share your feelings and fears with the one you love. I recommend that transsexual couples who are serious about their relationship take the time for couples counseling or enrichment classes. Maintaining any relationship over time takes a lot of work and cooperation on the part of both partners.

In my experience, the spouses of many transsexuals show an unexpected degree of love and understanding. Many still deeply love their transsexual spouse, and while they may not fully comprehend the need for change, they patiently work for their present or former spouse's happiness, sometimes even providing financial and emotional support throughout a transition which, by its nature, often precludes their later involvement.

I am a preoperative transsexual. At what point should I tell my new sweetheart about my situation?

There is no universal answer to this question, which raises issues of honesty as well as privacy. How do you balance a potential partner's reasonable need to know who you are against your need as a transsexual to maintain a degree of anonymity? In general, most transsexuals with whom I have worked do not go around making public announcements about their situation. They do, however, tend to bring up the issue as it becomes relevant.

Although some transsexuals will let anyone they intend to go out with know about their condition before the first date, most wait until they are sure that the relationship has a future and that they are genuinely interested in the person as a partner. Some will begin by dropping hints or bringing up topics related to tolerance, noticing how the prospective partner responds. If they encounter a degree of sensitivity and compassion, they proceed; if not, they move on.

When the partner is told, the initial response is often one of anger or betrayal over having been unfairly led along. Many partners disappear when they find out. Others, however, are able to cope with their anger or other feelings, and decide to stay in the relationship, some for a short period, others for the long term:

"I was very angry at first, but I finally realized that I had fallen in love with the person, not the sexual identity. It is true I'd never have chosen this, but given the circumstances, I'm staying for now."

The situation for married transsexuals is similar. Some spouses remain friends; a few even stay married. This has lead to interesting situations in which, for instance, a male-to-female transsexual has surgery and remains married to the wife—

a case of two females, one biological and the other transsexual, who choose to remain legally married.

Some observers have questioned such relationships. Why would a person go through the sex-reassignment process only to remain with someone of the same gender? Such questioners should remember that everyone is not heterosexual, and know that a small minority of postoperative transsexuals do choose mates of the same gender.

My advice is to listen to your own heart, and consider the feelings of your potential partner, when deciding whether to disclose that you are a pre- or postoperative transsexual. As corny as it may sound, the Golden Rule often works best: treat others as you would like to treated.

My fifteen-year-old son has been in analysis since he was four. Why, after ten-plus years of therapy, does he still want to be a girl?

It has been my experience that all the money, all the therapy, all the prayers and all the self-punishment parents can heap on themselves will not undo the transsexual web. Although there are countless cases of individuals who have been through intensive psychotherapy and psychoanalysis, often with highly experienced therapists, I am not aware of a single instance in which therapy, or treatment of any kind, has changed the internal demands of an adult transsexual. Add to this countless loving interventions by various clergy and spiritual leaders, all of which, after many hours of prayer and meditation, have resulted in the same outcome—the sorrowful, yet unchanged, heart of the transsexual.

My daughter was molested when she was three years old. Is that why she wants to be a boy?

I have treated and evaluated hundreds of transsexuals, and they have exhibited no higher incidence of child molestation than exists among the general public. Yes, it is true that child molestation affects different people in different ways. And yes, it is possible for such traumas to contribute to a variety of mental problems, including gender confusion. But it is unlikely, in my view, that such events would in themselves result in a diagnosis of transsexuality. (I know of no case in which such a single circumstance has led to the permanent condition of transsexuality.)

Temporary gender confusion, created or exacerbated by sexual abuse, must, of course, be properly evaluated and treated. The question of whether or not the individual is truly transsexual may be resolved in the course of treatment.

I am a female-to-male transsexual who has recently completed surgery. How do I approach my employer about using the men's bathroom?

Going to the bathroom in America is gender specific behavior, and therefore high on the behavioral priority list for transsexuals. Not only should transsexuals use the bathroom appropriate to their gender choice, most gender treatment teams *require* their patients to cross-dress and live as a member of the opposite sex for a significant period of time. Of course, this includes using the appropriate bathroom.

In most instances, the transsexual has gone to work for a period of time in his or her biological birth-gender role. In order to reasonably expect an employer to shift gears and accept you as a transsexual—with everything this condition entails—there are a number of things you must first have in place:

1. You should be in a legitimate gender program, having been diagnosed and accepted into therapy.

2. You should be very comfortable with your chosen new gender and with your cross-dressing. If you are not at ease with yourself, it is unreasonable to expect anyone else to be. You should have no serious doubts about your choice, since it may not be reasonable to ask your employer to allow you to return to your former dress and behavior after he has gone out of his way to accommodate you in your new identity.

3. You should be an employee in good standing. If you are already on probation for sloppy work or have constantly abused your sick leave, I would recommend you improve your work image before expecting others to accommodate you.

4. You should have a letter from your gender team or therapist explaining the medical necessity of changing your

work attire, choice of bathroom facilities, etc. The letter should invite the employer or personnel manager to address questions to these professionals.

You are likely to have less difficulty with government or other large-scale employers, since they are more likely to be familiar with the various sex-discrimination laws. It is my experience that employers who are treated with respect are much more likely to show respect to their employees (and vice-versa). I am aware of many instances in which the transsexual was able to stay at his or her job before and after sex-reassignment surgery.

If you do choose to make the transition while retaining the same job at the same work site, you must expect to experience a period of uneasiness and adjustment on the part of management, co-workers and supervisors. Remember, you are not the only one for whom this situation is new. Your colleagues are going to be naturally curious, and some patience on your part is a good idea. Over time, if you continue to be a good employee and co-worker, almost everyone will come to accept you. The novelty will wear off, and you will become just another face at work.

It is not unusual, however, to have one or two people who strongly resist accepting you. Sadly, that's life. While you do have the right to be treated with respect at your place of work, there is no guarantee that everyone will like you.

How do you know whether to call a transsexual "he" or "she"?

This is a practical problem that has confronted therapists and support staff at clinics and hospitals for decades. I usually instruct my staff to adhere to the following guidelines:

- If a person presents herself in traditional female clothes, she should be referenced by feminine pronouns.
- If a person presents himself dressed in traditional male clothing, he should be referenced by male pronouns.
- If a person verbally presents as a male or female, this supersedes clothing and that person should be referenced by the gender pronoun with which he or she verbally presented.
- If the transsexual has filled out any paperwork, address the transsexual by the name he or she has listed.
- If in doubt, simply ask, "What do you prefer to be called?"
- Similarly, if the transsexual objects to a name or pronoun, simply ask, "What would you like to be called?"

After you have known or worked with a transsexual for a period of time, pronouns are seldom an issue.

PART 3:
PHILOSOPHICAL, PSYCHOLOGICAL AND SPIRITUAL ISSUES

How confident are you that transsexualality is a reality? Do you have any ethical or moral qualms about what you do?

When I first began working with transsexuals, most of my work was in diagnostics and psychological testing. I was pretty sure that those who called themselves "transsexuals" were really effeminate homosexuals, or transvestites, or acting out some other fetish. Even today, as I sat in my office interviewing a new case, a male-to-female 26-year-old transsexual, I was again amazed that this particular subgroup of gender-disordered persons has come to be so well defined.

Over the first few years of training, I began to notice that the transsexuals I was seeing came from every walk of life, from every continent, every income level and every religious background. (I was seeing people from little villages who had never heard of transsexualism.) Part of what convinced me of the reality of transsexuality as a clinical phenomenon was the number of patients identifying themselves as such—more than five hundred to date. It was also the consistency and reliability of what I was hearing. The general presentation, the basic information, and the nuances of attitude and belief became familiar, even predictable. While the individual stories varied, there were undeniable common threads running through these personal-life narratives.

How often, for example, I encountered the following question: "Doctor, I fantasize about having my penis ripped off in a car accident. Am I crazy?" This represents a common "wish fulfillment" fantasy for male-to-female transsexuals, where the dream or fantasy is a desired state or outcome. Diagnostically, the most interesting element in such dreams or fantasies is the absolute absence of classic castration anxiety. Whereas the heterosexual, homosexual or bisexual person is apt to experience considerable anxiety when confronted with the notion of injury or surgery involving their sexual organs, the transsexual is not put off by graphic descriptions of surgical castration or hysterectomy. This vividly displays how relevant is the transsexual's individual response to proper diagnosis: it is one thing to want to dress up or act like the opposite sex; it is quite another to wish for the excision of your genitalia.

I also searched for strong elements of what psychotherapists call "secondary gain," which occurs when a patient receives an indirect and positive benefit from his or her pathological behavior patterns. Such patterns are often self-perpetuating, tending to maintain the pathological behavior, often in subtle ways. A common example of secondary gain involves the sickly parent whose only child remains single in order to see that he or she is properly cared for. The attention that the parent receives from the child is called "secondary gain." It is a secondary benefit to the primary illness, hypochondriasis. (The child is similarly rewarded with the belief that he or she is a "good" child.)

My evaluation of transsexuals does not typically uncover significant pathological secondary gain. Most transsexuals wish merely to become themselves and blend into the fabric of the community. In general, they do not seek notoriety. While they may, like most of us, crave a degree of attention and affection from their fellow human beings, they do not wish to be identified as a "he-she" or otherwise notorious freak.

For nearly two decades I have been confronted with the permanency of the transsexual phenomenon in those who have been properly diagnosed. Its apparent immutability has lead me to perceive it as a naturally occurring biological anomaly. I have observed years of analytical therapy rendered impotent by this phenomenon. I have watched as massive positive and negative reinforcements wash over the transsexual's psyche like so many drops of rain.

So, in answer to the first part of your question: yes, I do believe—without any reservations—that this phenomenon, affecting hundreds of thousands of individuals, is real.

The second part of your question focuses on my ethics, which you suspect are faulty, presumably because I participate in a process that assists transsexuals in obtaining reassignment surgery. (Ironically others may perceive me to be unethical because I will not write a letter recommending a psychotic transsexual for reassignment surgery.)

For my part, I have fully accepted the professional role of helping this group of gender-disordered patients find a satisfactory means of getting past their profound dissatisfaction with their birth gender. If life were perfect and fair, the transsexual phenomenon would not exist. However, given the actual state of affairs, it seems not only proper but essential that professionals help transsexuals examine their transsexuality and, when appropriate, recommend them for surgery. My role is to provide the evaluation and therapy—over decades, if necessary—that will bring transsexuals (or non-transsexuals) to the crossroads at which they can accurately perceive their own reality and thus make their own informed decisions. I have never thought of myself as making the final decision. My role is to state whether, to the best of my knowledge, the patient is a transsexual who is capable of deciding whether he or she wishes to be sexually reassigned. I see myself as offering a second opinion, although at this juncture my professional opinion has never differed from that of my patient.

It is important to note, however, that over the years hundreds of individuals who initially presented themselves as transsexuals have been able, thanks to the process of evaluation and treatment, to ascertain that hormone treatment or reassignment surgery was not the course they should take. They came to understand that while they were gender disordered, they were not true transsexuals. In the absence of a professional like myself, these patients might have chosen to undergo inappropriate transgender surgery.

It may surprise you to learn that I believe in God. I also believe that God knows more about transsexuals than anyone else. I am satisfied that God will deal fairly with me and with the transsexuals with whom I work. I believe, and I believe that most religions would concur, that it is morally sound to alleviate the suffering of such people, to help them to find hope and peace, and, where possible, to become whole.

I cannot tell you how you should feel, but I sleep well in the belief that what I am doing is necessary and good.

How do child, adolescent and adult transsexuals present themselves to the therapist?

Excellent question. Nearly everyone has heard the quote about feeling "like a man trapped in a woman's body"—or vice-versa. Rest assured, a five-year-old gender-dysphoric child does not give this answer when asked what the matter is. Behaviors, attitudes and verbalizations vary greatly with the age of the gender-dysphoric individual.

The transsexual's passage from childhood to adulthood is not a smooth, linear journey. It is characterized by rough starts and stops, tangential leaps and jerks, as well as by disappointing setbacks.

Children respond to their unhappiness in a manner consistent with being children. During play therapy, the five-year-old male-to-female transsexual may cry and ask to play with the baby doll. He will not say, "Listen, I'm really a girl—let's get on with the surgery." The young child will show his or her gender choice and dysphoria more by actions than by words. Choice of playmates, games, clothes and toys will give more diagnostic clues than will the limited verbalizations of children—although these should by no means be ignored.

As children enter into elementary school, their verbal interactions become more and more telling. They may, if the environment is safe, begin to share that they feel different from other children. However, if they do not feel safe, or if those around them express disapproval of their needs, they will often draw inward, hiding their feelings and pretending to be who they are not.

While the eight-year-old female-to-male transsexual does not understand the complexities of human sexual behavior and reproduction, she does know that standing up to urinate constitutes an important difference, and that it is something she desires. She realizes that the gender-specific attitudes of the people around her are somehow askew, that something is wrong and needs to be fixed. Like the younger child, the eight-year-old is likely to internalize and retreat, only to come out another day. Like the bar of Ivory soap, you can hold it underwater, but it will always float back to the surface. With children who are true transsexuals, their need to be themselves will resurface again and again.

Because society's allowances for adolescent "whims" give many young transsexuals the opportunity to dress unisexually, parents rationalize many developing cross-gender issues by blaming a too-liberal social environment. Unlike the five- and eight-year-olds, the teenager is experiencing dramatic hormonal and physical growth. The budding of breasts, the emergence of facial and body hair, menstruation, the shaping of physiques and figures—all this makes it impossible for the teenage transsexual to fully deny the physical trap in which he or she has been caught.

It is during this period that depression becomes a regular part of the transsexual's life. It is not that depression does not effect young transgender children, but that the depth, frequency and duration of the depression is more acute in adolescence. While the younger child may worry about gender issues from time to time, teenagers are cognitively equipped to sustain their concerns. Their confusion and anger may lead to significant acting out, to alcohol and drug abuse, as well as suicide attempts. Many transsexual teenagers experiment with homosexuality to see if this is who they are. Others try to make heterosexuality work for them, or maintain a certain stand-offishness, avoiding sexual expression with both males and females.

In the course of the transsexual's early adulthood, three paths are most commonly followed: they bury their feelings in the effort to be a "real" biological man or woman; they drown their problems in alcohol and other chemicals; they enter into therapy, which may result in an understanding of the source of their gender confusion. Some will find that they are, indeed, transsexuals and begin the process toward surgery.

At what age may a person be regarded as a candidate for surgery?

It is my professional opinion that the diagnosis of transsexuality, as distinct from a diagnosis of gender confusion or dysphoria, cannot be reliably made until adulthood. For this and other reasons—and although I agree with those who believe that children and adolescents experiencing gender dysphoria should be given a broad range of expression and plenty of therapy—I believe that a child should never be considered for surgery, or any other procedure that is not totally reversible. It is imperative, however, that the gender-confused or transsexual child receive therapy as soon as the problem has been identified. This will help the child through the difficult early years, as well as prepare him or her to eventually make a decision regarding surgery.

It is equally important to recognize that no matter how loving the parents or understanding the physicians, this is a decision that can only be made by the transsexual—again, as an informed adult. While transgender issues are upsetting to parents and threatening to some medical professionals, the individual's freedom to be who he or she is must be protected during childhood.

If the child is truly a transsexual, all the king's horses and all the king's men will not make him otherwise. Still, premature action by well-meaning family members may destroy an otherwise promising life.

How does the young child experience transsexuality?

Nearly everyone—including Mom and Dad—tends to treat male and female children differently. Researchers have pointed again and again to the subtle and not-so-subtle ways in which the genders receive different responses from grown-ups. Day in and day out, the young undiagnosed transsexual is confronted with behaviors and attitudes that are in absolute contradiction to his or her internal self. Although no two individuals are exactly alike, I have noticed striking similarities across cases.

Consider Bobby, a biological male, now Bobbie, a post-operative female. Bobby never enjoyed playing with traditional boys' toys—the baseball and bat, the little fort with the plastic cowboys and Indians, the toy guns and swords that gathered dust until they were given to the Salvation Army. Instead, he played with his sister's, or the neighbor girl's, toys. He could spend hours side-by-side with the girls, playing "house" or "tea party." When Bobby reached ten years of age, the girls would seek him out to fix their hair and talk about make-up. On weekends, they would play beautician. For those moments, at least, Bobby's young life was filled with joy.

Unfortunately, while Bobby always seemed to fit in with the girls, the boys would taunt him unmercifully, calling him "sissy" and other degrading names. Other parents in the neighborhood, who perceived Bobby as harmless if odd, would suggest from time to time that perhaps he needed a stronger father figure, or that he should join the Cub Scouts. They failed to take into account the fact that Bobby's father was stereotypically macho in speech, dress and behavior, or that the family had tried in vain to bribe Bobby into the Scouts.

Bobby reports that he did not realize he was a boy in the biological sense until he was about three years old. He lived in his child's mind as though he were a girl. He became upset when, playing "doctor" with several of the neighborhood children, he discovered how his body differed from that of the other little girls. He remembers being confused. It just didn't make sense to him that he was going to grow up to be like his older brother or his father.

Bobby had an active dream life as a young child, with "good dreams" of being a princess or an everyday housewife. His favorite dream was waking up to find that he had really been a girl all along, and that his male identity had been a terrible nightmare. His physical gender was a nightmare to him.

As Bobby grew older, his mood darkened. He dreamed that while playing with a group of other girls in the school yard, several big boys from the sixth grade ripped off his dress and revealed him for what he was—a boy and a freak. Bobby would wake up from such dreams covered with sweat, his body trembling, the tears flooding down his cheeks. It would be years before Bobby would share the content of these disturbing dreams with his parents.

While Bobby could not seem to control his dreaming, he could control his fantasies. In his imagination, he would travel to a world where the sun always shined, the sky was forever blue, the flowers always fragrant, and where Bobbie, the little girl, could play eternally with a group of girlfriends. At school, he began to lapse into waking dreams more and more often, a source of concern to his teachers and counselors.

To the family's dismay, even before puberty Bobby began using make-up. Although his use of make-up in public was tasteful and minimal, it nonetheless worried the family. His mother and father were sure that he was gay, and expected Bobby to confront them with this "news" at some point in the near future.

Fortunately, Bobby found a female counselor who took the time to understood him as no one else ever had. She realized that Bobby was a special child with a problem that he could not handle alone, and which even she found baffling. Bobby is convinced to this day that without the support of that counselor, suicide would have claimed another child victim.

Now consider Marian (today, Marvin), the middle child of three. She was a beautiful baby—blond hair, blue eyes and a smile for everyone. Momma dressed Marian in frilly pink-and-white dresses, and she was the apple of her daddy's eye.

During her early years, her Mom and Dad would comment casually to one another that she had more in common with William, her brother, than she did with Jill, her sister. As the years passed, her parents' casual observations evolved into a solid impression that caused them grave concern.

By age two, they could not keep a dress on Marian. A rough-and-tumble little tyke, she enjoyed being treated like a boy. At age three and four, Marian was climbing, scuffling, shooting stick guns and dressing as a pirate, complete with eye-patch and burnt-cork mustache.

Despite threats and spankings, as well as more creative punishments and rewards, Marian persisted in rejecting dolls, frilly lamps and bedspreads, and anything else that looked, felt or smelled feminine. Her preference for traditional boy's sports, games and toys continued, and her family gradually adapted.

Her parents recall vividly the day Marian, then about three-and-half, asked them when she would get her "peepaw." It took a couple of seconds before her parents realized that their little girl was serious. She had decided that it was just a matter of time before she grew a penis like her brother. Marian was to pursue this question for several more years, rejecting any suggestion that she was mistaken. Until she was about five years old, Marian was convinced she would one day awaken to find that she had grown a penis. It was around this time that Marian's mother and father realized that they would need professional help for the little girl they loved so dearly.

Marian loved her parents. She had tried many times to be a "good girl" and do things in a way that would please Mommy and Daddy, but she just couldn't seem to pull it off. Her child psychologist, while competent, had never diagnosed a transsexual and was naive regarding transgender issues in general.

As Marian grew older, she became more solitary at play and more isolated in her thinking. The actions and words of the people around her conflicted in almost every way with how she felt inside.

It was only in her euphoric dream and fantasy life that she could drop the unnatural shackles of her body and become "Marvin." She would soon enough graduate to highs that were both dangerous and addictive. She was a practicing alcoholic by the time she was fifteen.

Another oft-reported scenario is one in which the young child succeeds in repressing all expression of his or her inner self. Fantasy becomes the only means of conscious expression. In all such cases, I have observed that—under the pressure associated with repressing such inner feelings, coupled with the self-hatred associated with pretending to be what they are not—the facade eventually crumbles. As parents, friends and loved ones pick through the wreckage of the emotional lie, they discover a fragile human child starving to be loved and accepted for who he or she really is.

What are the adolescent years like for the transsexual?

Imagine having felt like a male since birth. How would you feel when breasts began to bud, when feminine lines come to dominate your silhouette? What if you have felt like a female since birth, and suddenly a full growth of beard emerges, your voice deepens, and erections have a way of appearing at the most inopportune times?

The middle- or junior-high-school years are particularly frustrating for the transsexual, who faces all the customary challenges, including the symptoms of physical maturation that accompany this age. The raging hormone changes that fuel uncertainty in the healthiest adolescents are even more confusing for the transsexual, who is rapidly developing the unwanted secondary sex characteristics of his or her birth sex.

Prior to this age, fantasy and denial have proven successful for many transsexuals. This period, however, slaps the gender-confused individual in the face with its physical reality. Issues of "dressing out" for gym class, to say nothing of showering, translate into frightening and upsetting experiences, just at the time when other teens are developing a sense of camaraderie. The usual genital joking and comparisons that abound at this age can be a horror for the transsexual.

It is during the middle- and high-school years that truancy becomes a major problem for many young transsexuals. In order to avoid the hassles in gym class and other gender-specific activities, they will often refuse to go to school. While home schooling—a necessity for a number of transsexuals I have known—may bring temporary relief, the adolescent is falling farther behind socially as he or she develops the habit of isolation.

It is at this age that thoughts of suicide are likely to enter the picture. Periods of self-doubt and depression, commonplace in adolescence, achieve tragic proportions in the transsexual. Most adolescents see themselves as being awkward or out of step with their peers; they are fearful that others will come to know their insecurities. On top of all this, the young transsexual must contend with a body he or she cannot accept.

Several pathways are typical of this age.

Jan initially withdrew into herself in the 8th grade, busying herself with her studies and working with her father on the farm. By accident she met, and was attracted to, a shy female classmate, with whom she developed a secret romantic and sexual relationship. For a while Jan thought of herself as homosexual—she was, after all, attracted to another female. Try as she might, however, she was unable to overcome her discomfort over her friend touching her genitals. Several relationships later, Jan was finally confronted with the fact that she not only did not enjoy her own body, but that she became confused or upset when her girlfriend would touch her "there." Jan ultimately did discover and accept herself, but this did not occur until college.

Byron, on the other hand, took a totally different approach, throwing himself headlong into a disastrous, if shortlived, heterosexual affair. Byron convinced himself that if he became a "super male"—he had the physique for it—he would learn to like females because, as he put it, "I am not a fag." However, like Jan, Byron was unable to adapt to or even minimally enjoy the lifestyle into which he had pushed himself. At fifteen, when he realized he was attracted exclusively to males, he became depressed and attempted suicide. (Byron was also quite homophobic, having adopted his family and peer group's views on the matter.) Fortunately, Byron entered therapy and, after some difficult work, was able to sort out his feelings and begin to accept who he really was. Byron, now Catherine, is a heterosexual transsexual and is reportedly happy in a long-term relationship.

Or take Sandy, who represents a broad group of transsexuals at this age. She accomplished the maximum required of her academically and the absolute minimum required of her socially. She spent time in her room reading and writing poetry, as well as doing volunteer work with young children. By avoiding contact with her peers, Sandy was able to delay for several more years her unavoidable confrontation with her own sexual dilemma. Sandy's group, perhaps the largest, is characterized by depression and much self-deprecation.

The last major group of adolescent transsexuals attempts to cope with gender confusion by turning to drugs and alcohol. Lonnie began raiding his parent's liquor cabinet at about thirteen. He was careful and meticulous at this stage, taking only a few ounces from each bottle, replacing the stolen liquor with water so it would appear that all was well. He was soon suspended, along with several of his cronies, for drinking beer in the school parking lot and for general disruptive conduct. Lonnie's parents went ballistic as they watched their honor student flunk every one of his classes. He was arrested for shoplifting a case of beer at a local convenience store.

While chemical dependency and alcohol may initially offer a refuge, they serve in the long run to extend the period of confusion, dysphoria and indecision. By his early twenties, Lonnie had tried several times to sober up, in and out of the hospital. Each time he appeared to be making progress, he would be confronted with apparently insoluble issues of gender.

In sum, the middle- and high-school years are a nightmare for many transsexuals—although for a few the very fact that they are a nightmare may provide a ray of hope. In recent years I have been encouraged by several cases of insightful, self-accepting parents who have managed to recognize the struggle their teens are experiencing. What a difference it can make in a young transsexual's life to find at home a safe refuge from the hostile world they otherwise face.

What is meant by the terms "superman" and "superwoman"?

These refer to a common phenomenon, experienced by well over half of my transsexual patients. They have dreamed about becoming a woman (man), prayed to become a woman (man) and planned over years to save thousands of dollars to finance the surgery they need to become a woman (man). Their every day and night is filled with hopes and dreams of becoming a member of the opposite sex.

As a result, it should come as little surprise that many evolving transsexuals exaggerate aspects of masculine or feminine behavior. After years of insecurity, when transsexuals finally start coming of age, they may overdramatize the concrete reality of their chosen gender. In terms of the psychological evaluation, it is not unusual for such individuals to answer nearly every test question in a gender-specific fashion. Such responses do not eliminate the transsexual candidate, but do suggest that the candidate does not yet have a mature self-image. Being transsexual does not mean the individuals must reject every aspect of themselves. It means, rather, that they will keep much of who they are. The changes they do undergo will not, in most instances, overshadow the many parts of themselves which they do, and should, wish to retain.

The mature transsexual, like the mature heterosexual or bisexual, should be able to recognize and accept the various male and female ingredients that make up his or her physical and emotional self. What counts is self-acceptance. Transsexuals have gone through incredible efforts to come to terms with who they are. It is shortsighted, and potentially handicapping, for them to fail to recognize the important principle that we are all really just human beings, with varying degrees of male and female traits.

What about depression and suicide among transsexuals?

Transsexuals are confronted by myriad frustrating, contradictory and depressing situations and experiences, and therefore should be depressed. I would argue that if they were not depressed, they would most certainly not be displaying a normal transsexual pattern. Often, it is depression and anger that help transsexuals maintain their focus and, in time, attain a positive resolution of their dysphoria.

Because suicidal thoughts and actions often accompany deep and persistent depressions, suicidal variables may appear more frequently in the backgrounds of transsexuals than of the general public. When I am working with a transsexual with a history of suicidal impulses or gestures, I explore with them the reasons for their thoughts and actions. If depression, anger and suicidal variables are related to gender dysphoria, they will most likely abate as the transsexual moves along the treatment path. Suicidal intentions tend to dissipate as people come to believe that a positive outcome is likely.

In my experience, once a transsexual has dealt with these issues, he is no more or less inclined to depression or suicide than anyone else.

In your experience, what kinds of biases do physicians and therapists bring to their work with transsexuals?

Like anyone else, doctors bring their own baggage to these issues. The first example of this I can recall involved a male-to-female transsexual who intended to continue a sexual relationship with a woman. In other words, she intended to lead a homosexual life post-surgery. I remember the gender team's discussion as to why a person would go through all the trouble of transgender surgery, then want to be a homosexual. It finally dawned on us that transsexuals are a mirror of the larger society, where a significant minority have a homosexual orientation. Most of the gender-team members were heterosexuals and were therefore showing a clear sexual bias, albeit unconsciously.

A second story is, I believe, even more intriguing. The team was confronted with a certain female-to-male transsexual, a case in which—to state it politely—the surgeons doubted seriously whether the candidate would make an aesthetically pleasing man. The reality that some people are pretty while others are not is a hard one for some plastic surgeons to accept. Remember, for most of their careers they have been striving for visually pleasing outcomes. It can therefore be difficult for them to commit to performing surgery on someone whose looks will not be appreciatively improved by the process.

The average psychologist, psychiatrist, primary-care physician and surgeon knows little or nothing about gender dysphoria or transsexuality. It is imperative that transsexuals convince themselves that they are seeing someone who has had experience in the diagnosis and treatment of such problems. If he or she lacks such experience, shop around. You do not want to work with a doctor who does not want to work with you.

Will doctors think I am not a transsexual if I refuse to take hormones?

While the decision not to take hormones will certainly be questioned, the inquiry will focus more on the reasoning behind the decision. I have worked with a number of transsexuals who are comfortable with their physical attributes and do not require any enhancement of their secondary sexual characteristics. A second group rejects hormones based on concerns regarding the very real long-term physical and psychological effects of using them.

I support all informed decisions by the transsexual to undergo almost any procedure, whether it be hormones, electrolysis or surgery. It is, after all, his or her body, and he or she should be assisted and supported in making an uncoerced decision. If your doctor insists that you take hormones, find another physician.

I am a candidate for sex-reassignment surgery, and I do masturbate. Does this mean I am not a transsexual?

The majority of transsexuals report that they have masturbated at least once. A significant minority report masturbating to orgasm occasionally, as the "physical need" becomes great. Fewer than five percent report masturbating "regularly" or "frequently."

Jamie reported masturbating nearly every week. He stated that he had a high sex drive, and that if he did not masturbate he would have nocturnal emissions, which he found distasteful. His masturbation technique, however, was unusual. He would put on tightly fitting pantyhose, lay on his back, spread his legs and rest a vibrator on his penis. As the vibrator brought him to climax, Jamie would fantasize that he was a woman and that the phallus-shaped vibrator was a penis entering his vagina.

In most instances, transsexuals find methods of masturbation whereby they do not touch their genitals. Using their own hand (or allowing another's hand or mouth) to stimulate their genitals is a form of gender acceptance, and this is intolerable. Shower massagers, vibrators, and various methods of rubbing or rocking the body are among the non-touching techniques employed. Individuals can be very inventive in finding ways to achieve an orgasm without giving gender recognition to their genitals.

As for transsexuals who are among the five percent that do masturbate regularly, it is imperative to talk directly and openly with your surgeons. If you have surgery it is unlikely that masturbation will ever be to you what it has been. No one can guarantee that you will be able to achieve a comparable level of sexual stimulation or orgasm after surgery. Because most transsexuals have a low or nonexistent physical sex drive, they risk very little in this regard. The small group who enjoy masturbation should ask many questions—and consider the answers carefully before committing to surgery.

Although I have very little interest in sex, I feel I am a very sexual person. Does that make sense?

What you are saying is true for most transsexuals—and for many non-transsexuals as well. Sexuality involves being fully a man or woman. It is the background, the narrative, the color and texture of a person's life. While the sex act lasts for only a short time, sexuality encompasses the entirety of who we are, every minute of the day. Sexuality is most alive within the mind and heart of the individual.

As Erica Jong writes in her novel *Fear of Flying*, "Love is more than a rub and a tickle." Sexuality begins in the mind and spreads throughout the body, warming the heart and freeing the spirit.

Why should I continue to see my therapist after I've completed surgery?

Between one-third and one-half of all people who undergo major surgery experience postoperative depression. The transsexual is no exception to this surgery- and anesthesia-related phenomenon. In addition, there may be a sense of anti-climax similar to that experienced by anyone who, after years of hard work, has finally attained his or her goal. This kind of "let-down" is normal, but if not attended to may result in a serious depression. Treatment often involves the development of new life goals, with specific milestones set up along the way toward achieving them.

Well over three-quarters of all transsexuals "disappear" after surgery, having chosen not to complete the last stage of the process. Some with whom I have spoken have expressed an overwhelming desire to get on with their lives, to leave the past—including therapy—behind. It is possible that some of them have later sought out therapy on their own, without my knowledge. I certainly hope so.

What about God? Will I go to hell for being a transsexual—especially if I elect to undergo reassignment surgery?

For a significant minority of transsexuals, the question of God is both important and troubling. I have worked with Catholics, Protestants, Jews, Mormons, Seventh Day Adventists, Christian Scientists and Jehovah's Witnesses. I have worked with individuals from societies in which they can literally lose their heads for undergoing sexual reassignment. After eighteen years of working with transsexuals, it is my judgment that the transsexual phenomenon occurs within every culture in the world.

Transsexuals from some religious backgrounds have grown up with the admonition that homosexuality is a mortal sin. Some of them believe that cross-dressing is also a sin, punishable by fire and brimstone. These individuals believe that they are putting at risk the future of their souls—facing not just the loss of family and friends, but the ultimate judgment of God, which may include spiritual annihilation. To confront, explore and challenge such beliefs takes incredible personal energy and faith.

I am not a priest, a rabbi, a minister or an authority on any faith. I do not pretend to be able to answer the transsexual's questions about God, Allah, Jehovah or any other deity. When a Catholic transsexual talks with me, I encourage him or her to seek counsel within the church. (There are understanding clergy working in most religions, sensitive and willing to listen.) If a patient believes in prayer or meditation, I encourage that person to pray or meditate, continuing to seek answers.

This is all occurring at a time when many religions are facing the possibility that many cases of homosexuality are determined at birth and are not the result of individual sin. I have found little evidence to support the theory that nurture or life experiences are the principal causes of homosexuality *or* transsexuality. To say that an individual "chooses" his or her sexual orientation may someday be regarded as being as silly as the flat-earth theory. Future generations may look back on our scientific and social naiveté with wonderment. ·

I believe that no person or religion has an absolute corner on the truth. Do people have a right to their own flavor of religious faith? Yes. Does that mean that their religion's doctrine is without error? Probably not.

I abide by the following guidelines regarding transsexuals and religious issues:

- I do not challenge or criticize my patients' beliefs.
- I encourage them to seek religious counseling, within the confines of their faith, from a qualified counselor.
- I encourage them to pray, meditate or otherwise participate in religious practice.
- I encourage them to talk with other transsexuals of their faith.
- I help them reflect on their issues, but never interfere with their decision.

Brian is representative of many individuals I've worked with. He went through pastoral counseling with his minister. They prayed together that God would take away his transsexual and homosexual feelings. They prayed and they prayed—and the feelings remained. Brian considered himself a good Christian. He was technically a virgin—had never, in fact, engaged in any form of homosexual behavior, which he considered a sin. While Brian longed to marry a man, he would only consider it after he became fully female.

Brian made peace with his God. Since his feelings remained constant, despite more than a year of prayer and counseling, Brian came to accept that this was, in fact, the road God expected him to travel. He decided to place his soul in the hands of a God who understood him and whose judgment of him was flawless (unlike that of the church).

Each transsexual's story varies, but I can attest to the fact that many take the fate of their souls quite seriously. The majority come to believe that by undergoing surgery they are merely correcting a birth error, and that God understands even when others may not. Many state that they cannot find any passage in scripture that directly addresses the issue of transsexuality.

I have worked with those who believe that while God does not condemn them for being transsexual, it is a sin to undergo surgery, to tamper with what God has created. When this is their decision, I support them with the same level of caring as if they had decided to pursue the surgical option.

My experience suggests that some religions have more difficulty with homosexuality than transsexuality. Many, however, do not understand the difference; they see them as one and the same. Other religions do not even care to look at the matter, regarding transsexuality as evil without going to the trouble of making an evaluation.

It is not my job to persuade or cajole anyone. The decision rightfully belongs only to the individual.

Will you go to hell? I do not know.

What do I believe? I believe God has not given the exclusive right to discern truth to any person or religion. I leave justice to God and encourage everyone to find his or her own way, as directed by his or her heart, soul and conscience.

The overwhelming majority of transsexuals do manage to resolve their spiritual issues.

Since I am talking about religion, this may be a good place to discuss the anger that I have often heard expressed toward God by transsexual individuals who feel that an injustice has occurred. They ask why a loving God would allow them to suffer in this way. How and why would God allow a person's biological gender to stand in stark contradiction to his or her emotional and psychological self?

Once again, the answer to this question requires some soul searching.

Lacey was a member of an evangelical group. Frustration, then outright anger, were her first responses to her church's answers—or lack of answers—to her dilemma. Lacey eventually got the name of a church leader in another state who had had previous experience with the problems she was facing. After talking to him, Lacey began to feel better about her own situation and the decision which she was moving toward.

Lacey has since become Larry. While Larry is not allowed to maintain a formal relationship with the church, he is at peace with his decision to undergo sex-reassignment surgery. He is pleased to know that a minority of the church leadership believes the day may come when he can return. If transsexuality becomes accepted as a kind of birth defect, Larry believes, the church may change its stance. In his heart, Larry believes that God understands, and that so long as he is attentive to God, he is in good standing with his faith. He does not believe church membership is necessary for salvation.

Mary had better luck with her church. She went through several years of pastoral and mental-health counseling, and is still an active member of her congregation. While her change of gender has not been formally accepted, her local church has quietly decided not to make an issue of her situation, or of her participation in church activities. Mary, now Mason, continues to work with the church in many ways. He prays for the day that the church formally accepts those who, like himself, hunger for a spiritual as well as a physical and emotional home.

PART 4:
PREPARATIONS

Cross-dressing: How does one begin?

Because everyone who cross-dresses does not decide to go through the transsexual surgery process, it is recommended that candidates progress a stage at a time, expanding their cross-dressing as they become more comfortable and assured of their direction.

While a smorgasbord of approaches have been employed, Michelle's is characteristic of many. Her early life involved dressing as dictated by her biological gender, and as enforced by her biological parents. Like many female-to-male transsexuals, she gravitated to "tomboy" clothes, or to the more masculine-cut female styles. On more than one occasion she "accidentally" and irreparably damaged the disgustingly frilly dresses and hats her mother would buy for her.

Like many young undiagnosed transsexuals, Michelle attained some level of success in shaping her parents' attitudes. Eventually they tired of the struggle and began, albeit begrudgingly, to provide her with gender-neutral attire.

During high school and early college, Michelle dressed androgynously. Her junior year in college, she began dressing as a man. As a senior, she began smoking small cigars, sporting a crewcut and showing a faint mustache. When she contacted my committee, she had been cross-dressing for years—since long before she knew what a transsexual was. Her period of transition was therefore relatively smooth and straightforward.

Samuel, whose case stands in stark contrast to Michelle's, grew up on a family farm. Since the Revolutionary War, the men in Samuel's family had joined the army when they were old enough, and many had gone to war. When Samuel was born, no one expected things would be any different. His grandfather celebrated the occasion by putting aside $250 for Samuel's first rifle, which he was due to receive on his sixth birthday.

Samuel swallowed his feelings and tried to toe the family line. He wore boy's clothes almost all his childhood, with one brief though significant interlude. At about thirteen, Sam secretly began wearing his sister's clothes when the family was out of the house. After a period of months, Samuel began to feel more adventurous. He stole several pairs of his older sister's panties and started wearing them under his regular underwear.

This continued for several months—until the accident. When Samuel broke his leg while doing his farm chores, his parents carried him to the small rural hospital. When the doctor came out to report that Samuel would be fine physically, the doctor also presented his parents with the pair of pink panties which they had cut off along with his other clothes.

Samuel's father was incredulous, and so upset that the doctor decided to keep Samuel overnight. Samuel's brother and sister came to the hospital room and gave him a tongue-lashing. They did not know exactly what had happened, but they had never seen their father in such a state. They told Samuel in no uncertain terms that whatever he'd done, he'd "damn well better never do it again."

And he didn't, at least not until he had joined the army, where he felt a kind of freedom he had never felt at home. On leave, instead of hanging out with the guys, Samuel went shopping—"for his sister," he said. He began to cross-dress at every opportunity. He met another cross-dresser, but parted ways quickly when homosexual possibilities presented themselves. It wasn't that Samuel didn't want a relationship with a man. He did. But he wanted his male partner to want him as a woman, not as another man.

Upon discharge from the service, Samuel knew he could never return home. Unable to directly confront his family, Samuel wrote them a letter telling them of his intention to settle in the city, at least for a while.

It was here that he came into his own. He found a therapist to whom he could confide his innermost feelings. He began cross-dressing on weekends at first, patronizing several gay bars. Although he was not yet ready to enter into an active sexual relationship, the patrons of the bars did tend to accept Samuel for who he was.

Before he began cross-dressing full-time, Samuel had his name legally changed to Tina. His computer training in the army helped him land his first civilian job as a woman. His therapist had suggested a large company, because such companies were less likely to discriminate against him if they discovered he was a transsexual. (It is not that large companies are more understanding, just more fearful of sexual-bias lawsuits. Since case law in this arena is still evolving, many companies will deal cooperatively with transsexuals who are good workers.) Tina proved to be an excellent employee and stayed at her job, cross-dressing full-time until her reassignment surgery was completed. She is now a supervisor at work.

Janet is representative of many who come from small towns, where everyone tends to know everyone else. In such a setting there is no such thing as "experimenting" at a local restaurant or bar. Anyone new becomes an instant topic of conversation. Faced with this difficulty, Janet began cross-dressing as soon as she got home from work. She also found it easy to dress as she wished when working outside in her flower and vegetable garden. She did not feel comfortable, however, going to church, which was the town's number-one social institution, or to the shopping mall, or to the movies, or to a restaurant.

Instead, Janet would drive nearly two hours to a city of half a million. She began by going to dinner with a friend, but soon found herself venturing out alone. She found the anonymity refreshing, and was able to shop, eat and socialize without much difficulty. She began to make friends, and less than six months later moved permanently to the city.

Using the city as a place in which to experiment had given Janet the opportunity to see, and feel, what it would be like to be a man full-time. Indeed, there is no way to know how it feels to dress like a man other than by dressing like a man!

Along with cross-dressing, what else can I do to disguise my birth sex?

For the male-to-female transsexual, it is not difficult to hide the genitals in loose-fitting female clothing. However, more is at issue here than outward appearance; the transsexual desires not only the outward appearance of a female, but the private, "underneath" appearance as well. He wants to look down at his pubic area and not see a penis and testicles.

Several techniques have been employed to hide the genitals. The most common approach is to tuck the penis and testicles down between the legs; tights or pantyhose are able, in some cases, to sufficiently secure the male genitals from view, as well as approximate the shape of female genitalia. A few pull the penis upward and pressed tightly into the abdomen, with pantyhose and various types of tape holding the penis in place.

A more sophisticated approach involves tying a silk cord or similar material around the bulbous tip (*glans*) of the penis and pulling it backward, so that the penis and scrotum (depending on size) fit into the groove of the buttocks. This cord can be secured to a waistband to maintain tautness. The male genitalia are often sheathed in a silken pouch, assuring that the penis will stay in place, even with vigorous movement.

Such techniques eliminate the frontal and side silhouetting of the genitals, allowing the transsexual to wear tighter-fitting clothes, including pantyhose, scanty bathing suits, short-shorts and certain styles in formal wear. If someone should place his hand in the pubic area, he may receive an impression of external female genitals—unless, of course, he attempts to probe too deeply.

Prior to hormone therapy or breast augmentation, most male-to-female transsexuals use a variety of padded bras and other accouterments readily available at any department store.

Further enhancements are attained in the same fashion as any woman would attain them: exercise and weight distribution to enhance feminine curves, stylish dress, hair treatments and the judicious use of make-up all help to make a person feel feminine, inside and out.

There are a variety of techniques to remove or minimize male body hair, including shaving, waxing, plucking, depilatory creams, hormone therapy and, of course, electrolysis. (When talking with an electrologist it is important to ask if she has treated transsexuals before, and, if yes, how many and what were the results. If you sense she is uncomfortable working with you, I recommend you move on. Also, it is recommended that you wait a while after beginning hormones, since you may need less electrolysis than you expect. Finally, given the concern over HIV, you should ask whether or not the electrologist utilizes disposable probes.) The latest method I've heard about involves the wearing of skin-colored tights to hide the hair on the legs, with pantyhose pulled over them to give a sheer appearance.

Many male-to-female transsexuals will wish to have their Adam's apples reduced in a surgical procedure called "thyroid-cartilage shaving." Rhinoplasty (i.e., a nose job), face lifts, tummy tucks and a variety of other elective plastic surgeries are also common.

Still, a woman is so much more than the absence of male genitals. Acquiring the right walk, talk, look, smile, attitude and heart are all essential parts of becoming female.

The bane of many female-to-male transsexuals is the breasts. Binding—the most frequent pre-surgical approach to hiding them—can be as simple as wrapping a length of scarf-like material around the breasts, or using a tight-fitting tube top. (While individuals with extremely large breasts are unable to utilize this technique, they are more likely to medically qualify for surgical breast reduction.) Prolonged wearing of binders, however, has commonly resulted in various breast rashes and occasional reports of the breast becoming distorted in shape.

As for creating the illusion of having a penis, this can be as simple as the pinning of a stuffed sock to the shorts in order to fill out the trousers. Others use an artificial phallus, athletic cup or stuffed athletic supporter to make this area more pronounced. Remember, it is important to look natural—not like an entry into the *Guinness Book of Records*.

By my observation, the most successful means to pass as a male do not involve body shape as much as they do the face. Many female-to-male transsexuals are able to grow a light mustache or beard; those on hormones are often able to grow as thick a beard as a genetic male. Nothing tends to engender acceptance as a male faster than appropriately groomed facial hair.

Most elect to have short uni-sexual or mannish haircuts. (The creation of a receding hairline can also add to the effect.) The hands can be enhanced by wearing a large, plain masculine ring. Masculine tattoos are also popular—although tattooing, like surgery, should not be entered into lightly.

While as a doctor I can't in good conscience recommend smoking, some female-to-male transsexuals do adopt typically male props such as the cigar and pipe. My advice is that if you like to smoke and are willing to accept the health risks, it may be effective in suggesting a masculine presence. If you don't enjoy smoking, forget it.

Exercise with a focus on appropriate muscle development can lead to emotional, as well as physical, enhancement. Here, as elsewhere, it is important to accept that the individual physique sets the upper limits of development in this regard.

While it is natural for such a person to want to explore one's masculine side, the more the transsexual grows to accept her feminine as well as her masculine side, the healthier and more natural she will be—and appear to be. As I have stated before, when you truly accept yourself, others will be more likely to do the same.

I have begun to experiment with cross-dressing, but find that I am not yet comfortable with my new—and evolving—sexual and social identity. How can I bring myself up to speed on dating?

Dating and other social skills are assimilated largely through observational learning—that is, by watching. I regularly suggest that people watch other people to see how things are done. If you want to know how to act at a party, at church, at a bar, at the opera or wherever, you can learn most effectively by observing what other people do. I recommend the following:

1. Carefully observe the behavior(s) you want to model.
2. Discuss with your therapist or with friends what is to be modeled, focusing on the actual details, as well as on any fears or concerns you may have.
3. Re-enact in fantasy what is to be modeled. Techniques such as hypnosis and guided imagery can be very helpful here, enabling the individual to live out each detail in his or her imagination. This greatly helps to reduce anxiety and eliminate fears.
4. Plan what is to be modeled, and how. Where will you do it? With whom? At what time? No detail is insignificant.
5. Now, actually perform the planned behavior.
6. Review the outcomes and accompanying feelings with your therapist and/or close friend(s).
7. Start again at number one.

Just as a little girl learns to jump rope by watching and remembering, so transsexuals learn to conduct themselves in social situations by observing movements, verbal phrases, facial expressions and other behaviors that can be incorporated into their repertoire of interpersonal skills. It is not unusual for individuals to exaggerate their newly acquired skills. Natural integration takes time, patience and practice.

The same is true when applying cosmetics. No one is born knowing how to do it. People learn by observation and by reading, as well as by trial and error. There are classes, videos and books on the subject. Some transsexuals hire a professional to help them get acquainted with the right colors and applications for their skin, build and physique. Clothing consultants can be helpful for those who need help building their wardrobe and "look." A well-planned wardrobe can play up the physical assets you wish to emphasize, while downplaying your figure challenges.

In therapy, role playing can be used to teach many skills. With a therapist (or friend), a transsexual may practice asking, or being asked, for a date without fear of failure or discovery. With today's technology, he or she can videotape the role-playing exercise and critique it before trying it again. This allows the transsexual to safely practice specific behaviors and verbal interactions. Videos are available to teach everything from ballroom dancing, to modeling, to make-up application, to proper etiquette.

Still, there is no substitute for actual experience. The only way to know what it is like to date a man is to date a man. The only way to know what it is like to kiss a woman is to kiss a woman. If you want to know what it feels like to wear a silk kimono on a moonlit night, there is only one way to find out. If you want to know what it feels like to be a postoperative transsexual, the best way, short of surgery, is to talk with postoperative transsexuals. The more you learn about your self—who you are, and who you are becoming—the more likely your decision will turn out to have been the correct one.

Can a transsexual have a baby of his or her own?

The intent of the question relates, I believe, to whether a post-operative transsexual can actually inseminate a woman, or conceive and carry a child to term. In both cases, the answer, of course, is no. However, a number of transsexuals have had children prior to making the transition, and a few transsexuals with whom I have worked have had their eggs or sperm frozen so that they could later have a child carried to term by a surrogate mother. Actual genital transplantation, with preservation of the reproductive apparatus, while discussed theoretically by some surgeons, is still a distant prospect. In some cases, transsexuals have developed close relationships with relatives or friends who have children, and are able to participate in raising them.

While these solutions are far from optimal, many transsexuals—like many barren non-transsexuals—must use one or more of these paths to explore and express their maternal or paternal selves.

What about adoption?

I am aware of at least one adoption of a child by a female-to-male transsexual and his biologically female wife. I am not aware of any legal precedents making such adoptions invalid or illegal. I would advise the questioner to seek legal counsel in the state in which he or she intends to adopt. It is important to see that the birth certificate has been changed to reflect the new gender—and that the couple possesses a valid marriage certificate—before appearing before the adoption board and/or judge.

Because you are a transsexual, everyone involved in the adoption decision will scrutinize you much more closely than they would a "normal" adoptive-parent candidate. It will be helpful if a few years—the more the better—have transpired since the completion of the sexual-reassignment surgery. It is even more important that you have shown good citizenship, maintained a steady job with good evaluations and have unequivocal letters of recommendation from several members of your gender team, or from other psychologists.

It is vital that one be clear about the principal issue here. The issue is finding appropriate placement for a child, not expanding the rights of transsexuals. The transsexual adoption candidate should be as concerned as the adoption professionals that the right decisions be made for the welfare of the child. The transsexual, in other words, should possess the characteristics of a good parent and provider.

Are the rights of transsexuals important? Absolutely. It is my belief, however, that the best way to make gains in this arena is for transsexuals to do a superb job in preparing to become parents. There is no room here, transsexual or no transsexual, for an "entitlement" mentality. Just because you have suffered does not justify special treatment by the adoption board.

How do I get my birth certificate and other legal documents changed to reflect my new gender?

I am not an attorney or a legal specialist. While I will share with you information relevant to this question, it is imperative that you seek legal counsel in your own state or jurisdiction. My comments are intended only for reference.

Most transsexuals begin with a name change, which is relatively painless and inexpensive. In most states you may file the papers yourself, although in some states you must appear before a judge. If you do not wish to appear in person or speak for yourself, you should find a competent attorney to handle the name change. (How do you find a competent attorney? Get a referral from your primary-care physician. Get a referral from an established transgender team. Get a referral from another transsexual. Talk with someone who is a satisfied customer. I have heard of people paying anywhere from $100 to $600 for a name change. Be a good consumer.) You may also wish to use the lawyer to change your social security, birth and employment records, as well as other significant papers.

In each of these cases, the court's primary concern is to thwart persons attempting to defraud others by assuming aliases or changing their names. Once it is clear that there is no intent to defraud, the name change should go smoothly.

After your name has been legally changed, you may apply to have the name on your birth certificate, driver's license, social security records and other legal documents changed. While most of the relevant agencies will offer no resistance to the name change, few if any will agree to change the birth gender as originally listed. Most will only change the sex shown on the birth certificate or other document after completion of surgery has been verified by a letter from the surgeon or other member of the gender team.

In my experience, many cross-dressing transsexuals are fearful of being stopped by a policeman and asked to present a driver's license with a photo showing the wrong gender. Such cases have only been reported to me two or three times. If the individual conducts himself in a reasonable and respectful manner, his explanation is likely to be accepted. If you are in therapy with a team acquainted with the legal issues, they will often write a brief letter stating your status as a transsexual candidate, and that the cross-dressing is an integral part of the treatment. I am aware of no instance in which the following letter was not sufficient to handle the situation:

[Date]
RE: John Smith, alias "Jane Doe"
To Whom It May Concern:
Please be advised that "Jane Doe" is a transsexual candidate and is in therapy with the [name of the program or committee]. The medical and psychological treatment requires that "Jane" cross-dress as a female all the time. This may also require that "Jane" utilize the bathrooms assigned for females.

I appreciate any help or consideration you may afford my patient "Jane Doe." If you have any questions at all, you may call me any time of the day or night at _____.

Sincerely,
Gerald T. Ramsey, Ph.D.
Licensed Clinical Psychologist

On a personal note, about half of the transsexuals with whom I have worked have chosen names that maintain some connection to the name they were given at birth. Charles may become "Charlene," James "Jamie" and so on. Others prefer to be known by their initials. A significant minority, however, do change both first and last names, seeking to extend the process of change to erasing affiliation with their family of origin.

Why should I have to go through a committee to have plastic surgery on my genitals? I didn't need anyone's permission to get my nose job!

You do not, in fact, need permission from a committee to have sex-reassignment surgery. If you have the money, there are surgeons around the world who will compete to perform plastic surgery on your genitals, no questions asked.

I do not recommend seeing such doctors under any circumstances. Two old clichés are true here: "You get what you pay for" and "If it sounds too good to be true, it probably is." Legitimate sex-reassignment programs have developed valuable protocols and procedures, and have enlisted the support of some of America's finest medical centers. While such requirements do add to the expense of transgender surgery, they also provide a higher level of security and protection for the patient.

There are legitimate clinical and medical/ethical—to say nothing of legal—reasons to require a through evaluation. Clinically, the best predictor of the future is the past. The best way to know what it is like to be a female is to live continuously as a female. This takes time. The longer the period of exploration and experimentation, the more confident the individual and his or her team of doctors can be. If the experimental period goes poorly, then further steps in the direction of sex-reassignment are not indicated. If the experimental period goes well, then both team and candidate progress to the next level.

Legally, any surgeon operating on transsexuals who has not solicited the active involvement of qualified mental-health professionals is placing herself at great risk. Imagine a courtroom scene in which Doctor X admits to having operated on the genitals of an individual whose only recommendation for surgery was financial, i.e., he or she had the cash. Imagine that sufficient blood flow was not realized, and the neo-phallus became necrotic and literally fell off. The transsexual has sued the surgeon.

That surgeon is going to have a difficult time with jury or judge and, from my perspective, *should* have a difficult time. One would have been negligent to operate on a transsexual who was not properly diagnosed, treated and recommended for surgery by an experienced mental-health specialist.

Like it or not, if you want genital surgery, inorder to ensure getting a competent surgery team, you are going to have to jump through any number of "hoops." You will most likely resent these procedures at first. However, by the time you are ready to undergo surgery, you will most certainly realize how crucial most of these steps have been toward attaining a positive outcome.

In general, what steps are followed by gender committees?

While the criteria and time requirements may differ from committee to committee, the following ten steps will almost always be required in one form or another. The steps are listed in the order in which they are generally taken. It is not unusual, however, for a transsexual candidate to have already taken the steps out of sequence. For example, someone may present who has been on hormone drugs for years, without having completed any of the preparatory steps.

So while it is optimal to have followed each step, in some instances it is not possible to retrace them. In the case just mentioned, rather than take the transsexual off medication he has been taking for months or years, the team evaluates him according to the remaining criteria.

Treatment for any psychological problem or disorder begins the moment the individual decides that he or she is going to seek help. Many transsexuals begin evaluating themselves years before they formally enter therapy of any kind, and have thus completed years of self-diagnosis and partial resolution of their psychological difficulties before crossing the doorstep of a professional.

STEP 1: *Evaluation and diagnosis of transsexuality by a trained clinical psychologist or board-certified psychiatrist. This evaluation should include standard psychological testing, as well as an I.Q. test.*

Diagnosis must be made by a mental-health professional who is both experienced and competent. While a professional from another field may diagnose transsexuality, such a diagnosis is fraught with potential liability.

Testing is generally completed by a clinical psychologist, and takes four or five hours to complete. (The report and results will also be useful to the transsexual's primary therapist, especially if the therapist practices in a different geographic area and will have little subsequent contact with the committee.) An I.Q. test should always be included, to assure that the individual being evaluated has at least a minimum level of general intellectual functioning. Unless the transsexual can make an informed decision, no surgical or hormonal therapy should be considered. I cannot imagine an instance in which a non-competent transsexual should be considered for surgery.

STEP 2: *Individual therapy to assess and treat the transsexual, to continue for a period of three to twelve months before taking the next step. Part- or full-time cross-dressing begins at this point, or earlier.*

Because most transsexuals do not live near the GID committee, the transsexual's primary therapist will play a crucial role in the treatment. The therapist must be willing at some point to write a letter stating that she recommends surgery and that, in her professional judgment, the individual is a transsexual. She must further state that she understands fully the process and risks, and feels that her patient will benefit from the procedures. Most teams require an unequivocal diagnosis from one or two qualified therapists other than the principal recommending therapist.

It is essential that the transsexual seeking therapy discuss with his or her therapist the eventual requirement of a letter of diagnosis and recommendation. I know of several transsexuals who have undergone therapy for years only to find out that the therapist never intended, under any circumstances, to write a letter recommending surgery. In these instances, the therapist believed that transsexuality could be cured with talk therapy and that surgical intervention should never be employed. Where this has occurred, the committee has required the transsexual to find another therapist and continue sessions for a specified period of time.

Transsexual candidates should be encouraged to interview prospective therapists prior to formally entering therapy. A second option is to have a licensed therapist familiar with transsexuality interview the prospective therapist on the transsexual's behalf. While it is imperative that the chosen therapist have an open mind regarding transsexuality as a diagnosis, that does not mean the therapist should grant automatic approval. It does mean he or she should be willing to write a letter for surgery *if appropriate*. I advise against seeing any therapist who will not openly discuss this important issue with you prior to entering into therapy.

STEP 3: *The transsexual is presented to the committee or team of specialists for acceptance into the program. Acceptance does not guarantee they will receive hormones or surgery. It does mean that they appear to have legitimate transsexual or other transgender issues with which the committee believes it can be helpful. Following acceptance, some committees will refer to their new client as a transsexual "candidate."*

GID committees typically include one or more plastic surgeons; a urological surgeon; a micro-surgeon; a gynecologist; an endocrinologist; and at least two psychotherapists, clinical or board-certified.

To my knowledge there is no state or national licensing or certification of GID committees or doctors. Any legitimate GID team would be happy to discuss their specific credentials, the history of the team, and the number of surgeries completed. (The Harry Benjamin Society (see end of Part V) will provide you with the names of any number of teams.) At a minimum, the members of the team should be licensed in their state and boarded in their surgical specialties. All team members should be experienced or supervised by a team member who is qualified and experienced.

There are many fine sex therapists who know absolutely nothing about transsexuals. In the final analysis you must use your judgment. Ask plenty of questions. If you are not satisfied with the answers...GO ELSEWHERE! This is too important a decision to be rushed.

STEP 4: *The transsexual's cross-dressing moves from part-time to full-time, at home and at work.*

If full-time cross-dressing isn't happening already, now is the time to begin. Cross-dressing is the chief way in which transsexuals are able to experience presenting themselves to the world as a person of the opposite sex. No hormonal or surgical interventions should be considered until the transsexual is actively cross-dressing. While there are many potential excuses for not cross-dressing full-time, they must be ignored. Cross-dressing should occur during all work, social, religious, recreational, educational and other time. (It is during this phase that many transsexuals begin to expand their social lives.)

STEP 5: *The individual is interviewed and evaluated by each of the specialists. Some teams may have a Clinic Day on which the transsexual spends the day meeting and being evaluated by individual team members. The evaluation generally includes several physical examinations by medical specialists, which may include the taking of nude photographs.*

The physical examinations, while uncomfortable for many transsexual candidates, are an essential part of the evaluation. It is typical for medical specialists to conduct separate exams and compare observations at a later meeting. The surgeons in particular need to carefully observe the transsexual's build and body make-up to determine which techniques or procedures are most suitable. The examination also includes production of photographs or a videotape—standard procedure for many plastic surgeons—showing the individual and his or her pre-operative genitalia. From a general medical standpoint, a thorough physical examination is performed, with blood work that includes HIV testing. (While individuals are not always disallowed following a positive result, they will not generally be considered for participation without being tested.)

Clinic Days save the transsexual a tremendous amount of time and effort. (The alternative is to individually schedule with each physician and psychotherapist.) Another advantage is the excellent opportunity to informally meet individuals who are also just entering the process, as well as those who are farther along. Many individuals have developed close relationships as a result of such informal meetings, and have later helped one another emotionally and physically during recovery from surgery. (One sure way of learning about the trials and tribulations of surgery is to help someone else through the early days of recovery.)

STEP 6: *The gender committee, which meets and discusses the candidate after he or she has been evaluated by the individual specialists, now makes specific recommendations.*

If an applicant has met none of the therapy requirements, the committee may recommend a therapist; or, if surgery has been approved, the candidate may receive specific instructions about diet, medication, lab testing and so forth. The basic function of step six is to let transsexuals know where they are in the process, and with which, if any, medical or psychological issues they need concern themselves.

It is my observation that treatment teams are less likely to terminate transsexual candidates than candidates are to eliminate themselves from the process. Many drop out at step six because they do not want to complete the requirements necessary to continue. For example, the committee may recommend:

- a candidate refrain from using drugs or alcohol for a period of time—usually a year or more—and be actively working a twelve-step program;
- a candidate first resolve in therapy certain issues that relate directly to gender dysphoria;
- an obese candidate lose weight that may compromise surgery and recovery;
- other medical problems be resolved.

STEP 7: *If the transsexual has cross-dressed full-time for a specified period of time and is making good progress in therapy, he or she may begin hormone treatment, or have minor preliminary surgery.*

The amount of time a candidate spends in psychotherapy before beginning hormone therapy ranges from three months to several years, with many starting hormone therapy between month six and month twelve of psychotherapy. The advisability of hormone therapy should not be taken for granted. There is a tendency for many to recklessly assume that hormone intervention has no long-term effects, that they can just stop taking the hormones and everything will return to normal. The literature on long-term hormone use is still emerging (see Part V). Please discuss the possible side effects with your physician *before* beginning hormones.

Many transsexuals, fearing ridicule or rejection by their physician, buy hormone drugs on the street, deciding or guessing at the appropriate dosage. *Never take street drugs!* If you wish to explore various scientific studies relating to hormone use, please refer to Appendix B of this book, where a sampling of recent studies is listed. For additional information, talk with a medical reference librarian about conducting a literature search.

In terms of preliminary surgery, many transsexual candidates consider chest enlargement or reduction, as well as neck, hand and facial surgery.

STEP 8: *When the various procedures in step six have been completed— and when the candidate is well along in therapy, and has been deemed physically healthy enough to undergo major surgery—the team votes on whether to approve the candidate's request to undergo the decisive stages of sexual-reassignment surgery.*

These surgeries are irreversible, in part or whole, and may include: a complete hysterectomy, complete castration, bi-lateral mastectomy, and construction of the neo-vagina or neo-phallus. Most committees require a unanimous vote. While this may sound like a difficult hurdle, by this point in the process it is clear to everyone whether the individual is or is not an appropriate candidate. (Most inappropriate candidates have, by this juncture, already eliminated themselves.)

STEP 9: *Surgery and surgical touch-ups.*

Pre-surgical instructions should include a statement about the post-surgical touch-ups that are necessary in a majority of cases. Upon discharge, the transsexual receives important information about follow-up and recovery. It is essential to follow the surgeons' instructions. If the doctors say to stay out of work for five weeks, then stay out of work for five weeks. When individuals are tempted to move ahead too quickly, I remind them of how long the process has taken, of the cost to them already—emotionally, financially and physically—and of how a few more weeks of patience is very little to ask.

STEP 10: *Follow-up psychotherapy is strongly recommended— if impossible to enforce.*

It is important to deal with the postoperative depression experienced by many individuals, as well as with issues relating to the final stages of adaptation and acceptance of who they have come to be. Follow-up therapy should be seen as the final deposit on a new life.

Do the criteria for who is a candidate for surgery change from committee to committee?

Unfortunately, there are no universally accepted criteria. The best-known set of guidelines, although not used by everyone in the field, is published by the Harry Benjamin International Gender Dysphoria Association, Inc., or HBIGDA; a copy has been reprinted with permission at the end of the next part. It is my opinion that anyone receiving surgery should be required to meet or exceed these guidelines. (My own team's requirements exceed these requirements, particularly where it comes to the time frames for cross-dressing and surgery.)

Switching from one gender treatment team to another may, therefore, present difficulties. Because different gender teams have different criteria, you may have to retrace some steps or extend the timeline necessary to qualify for various surgeries. It is not wise for a clinic to vary its protocol, and I encourage you not to press the point—the outcome may not be in your best interests. Often, a transsexual who has completed all but the definitive surgery comes to us having discontinued therapy. Our team requires that the candidate con-tinue therapy right up to the surgery itself. We require a letter from the primary therapist stating that she is well acquainted with the patient and recommends the surgery without qualification. This criterion cannot be met if the transsexual has been out of treatment for a significant time. If the therapist cannot address your condition present, his or her letter carries little, if any, clinical relevance.

I understand the gender team will want a detailed sexual history. What does this involve?

While sexual activity is not commonly one of the most important variables in the daily life of the transsexual, it is nonetheless important to the diagnosis and understanding of the individual. Most gender teams utilize detailed questionnaires, interviews or both. Although the questions may seem intrusive at times, there are solid theoretical and practical reasons for thoroughly assessing this aspect of the candidate's life.

The psychotherapist is obviously going to be interested in early sexual experiences, both those observed by the patient and those in which the patient was a willing or unwilling participant. Incidents of incest, rape, and/or physical abuse of the individual by a parent or siblings are all important. Just as critical is the sharing of information indicating positive and appropriate early sexual/social experiences.

In filling out questionnaires or while being interviewed, I encourage the transsexual to be direct and honest. It is not helpful to exaggerate the positives or the negatives. Be yourself and share your feelings. If sex is dull and lusterless, say so. Do not romanticize or attempt to feed the therapist the kind of data you think she wants to hear. It's your life and your body. The more accurate and open you can be, the better able the team will be to help you.

You will be questioned specifically on each significant sex partner, whether homosexual, bisexual or heterosexual. (If you rate yourself "asexual," questions probing into this choice will abound.) In terms of each relationship, you will be asked: How did you feel? How satisfying was the experience, emotionally as well as physically? How long did the relationship last? Were you in love? What attracted you to this individual? Why did you terminate the relationship? Very detailed questions will be asked relating to every variety of sexual activity, including oral and anal sex, masturbation, intercourse, foreplay, fetishes and fantasies. If you are shy, I suggest that you pick a difficult topic and jump right in. Remember that the therapist is asking these questions in order to gather information, not to embarrass you. The more you share with us, the better able we are able to assist you.

Why are pre-surgical visits with the gender team so important?

The purpose of such visits is to ensure that the transsexual-surgery candidate is prepared psychologically for surgery. Both literature and practice support the proposition that a person who is mentally prepared for surgery is more likely to have a positive outcome. The following are the issues I believe it is important to address when preparing a transsexual for surgery:

1. OPTIMISM: help create and maintain an atmosphere of honesty and optimism. The pre-surgical visit is the culmination of confidence-building and acceptance.

2. TRUST: a sense of trust in the individual surgeons, in the team as a whole, as well as in the procedures to be performed, is built up over the months—in some cases, years—leading to surgery. The team with which I currently work requires pre-surgery visits with all team members, when possible.

3. INFORMATION: the pre-surgical visit affords the transsexual the opportunity to reduce anxiety by asking and receiving answers to his or her questions. Team members seek to ensure that the transsexual has had ample opportunity to request and receive all the relevant information.

4. ANXIETY AND FEAR: after the other physicians have completed their pre-surgery visits, the psychologist or other mental-health specialist spends a quiet hour with the transsexual. Patients are encouraged to talk about their fears and concerns regarding surgery, outcomes and their future. If the transsexual has friends or relatives with him or her, they are generally invited to this session. The goal is to present a stable, reassuring picture of the upcoming surgery. Only twice in my experience has

surgery been postponed at this stage; in both instances, the candidate's anxiety was too intense to continue. The opportunity to express concerns and treatment with hypnosis (for relaxation) and/or medication are usually sufficiently effective to allow the surgery to go forward.

5. PAST SUCCESS: the patient is reminded during this process of his or her many successes over the past months or years. Some patients will have lost weight or stopped smoking in order to make the surgery possible. All will have overcome physical, emotional and financial obstacles.

Pre-surgical physical and mental-health visits are exactly the kind of procedure that make the difference between a quality program with excellent outcomes and one that trims too many corners. The pre-surgical visit is not intended as a last-minute attempt to discourage surgery. By this juncture, if an individual has undergone extended therapy and treatment, there should be no question as to the diagnosis. Enhancement of psychological preparedness is the principal purpose of this pre-surgical therapeutic process.

How commonly do transsexuals wind up regretting their decision to undergo surgery?

In my fifteen years of working with hundreds of transsexuals, not one of my patients has decided that he or she would like to reverse the process. I have, however, encountered individuals, operated upon elsewhere under the supervision of other gender specialists, who have come to our team requesting surgical reassignment to their original birth sex.

I believe there will be few such mistakes if the transsexual is treated by a legitimate gender team that follows guidelines similar to those stated earlier. Most mistakes will result from individuals not taking the time to complete the often frustrating, but necessary, discernment process. The parable of the tortoise and the hare applies here, with the same winner by a wide margin.

While I would like to see more follow-up studies, my recent review of the scientific literature continues to turn up positive post-surgical outcomes. Snaith, Tarsh and Reid (1993) studied 105 male-to-female and 36 female-to-male transsexuals in the Netherlands, and reported that "there is no reason to doubt the therapeutic effect of sex reassignment surgery." (They go on to note that results for the female-to-male transsexuals "compare favorably" with the results for male-to-female transsexuals.) Likewise, Pfafflin (1992) studied 295 transsexuals over a 30-year period and found only a "relatively small" number who regretted their decision.

While it is possible to surgically reassign a patient to their original sex, the qualitative outcome of this second reassignment would be diminished (when compared to the initial reassignment) in terms of function, aesthetics and genital sensation.

Finally, absolutely no such surgery should be undertaken without a serious return to the psychotherapy process, which may not have been appropriately explored the first time. It is essential that such an error not occur twice. Surgery should never be considered if the certain desire for transformation is not consistent over many years, as apparent to both the transsexual and the GID team. As harsh as it may sound, the pleadings of the transsexual or their loved ones should never be allowed to influence a team to prematurely commit to reassignment.

Do you encourage transsexuals to reevaluate their sexual orientations?

During the initial evaluation, it is customary to explore many areas, including a detailed sexual history. An individual's early experiences with both males and females are evaluated, as are instances of emotional and physical abuse, including rape. Specific questions regarding early sexual contact are important, as is the individual's sexual/social history in elementary, middle and high school and beyond.

More to the point, do I encourage individuals to consider "test driving" alternate lifestyles? If an individual presents with a strong religious belief that "alternate lifestyles" are evil, and if that individual has never had homosexual fantasies or experiences, I do not encourage an active exploration of the homosexual lifestyle. If his or her fantasy life is replete with images and suppressed feelings regarding gender identity, I recommend exploring this issue in therapy, although perhaps not in real life.

A person who has no moral or ethical constraints about exploring other sexual orientations is actively encouraged to explore the sexual possibilities, be that individual heterosexual, homosexual or both. It is obviously preferable that people explore sex involving their birth genitals before considering irreversible surgery. If they have surgery first, and have had virtually no sexual experience of the kind proposed, there is no way of predicting with any confidence that they will be happy.

For most of us, such experimentation with sexual situations will help to determine whether we will be happy as a homosexual or a heterosexual. But there may be additional nuances and implications:

1. A biological male-to-female transsexual who is sexually active with a heterosexual biological male may view

herself as being in a heterosexual situation—or as being in a homosexual situation, if she is with a female.

2. Similarly, a biological female-to-male transsexual who is sexually active with a heterosexual biological female may view himself as being in a heterosexual situation—or as being in a homosexual situation, if he is with a male.

3. If, however, either the male-to-female or female-to-male transsexual is in a relationship with a homosexual (someone who seeks to have sex with someone of the same gender), they typically deem themselves to be in a homosexual situation. How the situation is viewed rests largely with how the transsexual perceives his or her partner's emotional intentions.

I would never encourage someone who reports being happy with his or her sexuality or orientation to experiment with an alternative lifestyle. If an individual is basically happy, he or she should probably not complicate or compromise the situation. Just because you like the fantasy of swapping mates, for example, does not mean that you will like the emotional consequences. I am aware I am displaying a personal bias here, but it does seem to me that in seeking more, you may end up with less. Likewise, sexually inactive persons should not be harassed into "at least trying" dating if they do not wish to and have already come to terms with this aspect of their lives.

Why are therapy and surgery so expensive?

A heart transplant can cost as much as one million dollars, a week in prenatal intensive care $850,000, orthodontic braces $3,500, a plumber $75 per hour plus materials. The cost of services is high. That is the general answer to your question.

Now to the specifics. The average fee for psychotherapy in the United States is about $100 per hour. (It can range anywhere from $50 to $200.) Many therapists will negotiate a lower price if you have no insurance and pay cash. Fortunately, many insurers and health plans—including Medicare and Medicaid—cover a portion of each mental-health visit. In order to file a claim, it is necessary for the mental-health provider to make a diagnosis of transsexuality. If you are concerned about your employers finding out about your diagnosis, you must make sure they are not involved directly in the claims process.

Total surgical and hospital expenses can vary from as low as $6,500 to as high as $30,000. Some transgender surgical teams use as many as eight surgeons, physicians or nurses working together during the eight to twelve hours of surgery. Fees vary widely from specialist to specialist, from team to team.

The cost of hospital bed and operating room services varies widely. Most hospitals require full prepayment, or a large deposit, if they do not have a letter promising payment by an insurer. Hospital beds may cost anywhere from $600 to well over $1,000 per day. Operating-room costs currently range from hundreds to thousands of dollars per hour.

It is important to select a good surgeon and hospital. On the other hand, if you are paying cash most hospitals will give you a discount, some far steeper than you would guess. So negotiate. (The worst outcome is that you will pay full price.) Remember to shop both cost and quality—and if you must compromise, do not compromise on the credentials of the surgeon.

Why don't insurance companies cover transsexual surgery?

Although most insurers and health plans cover the psychological diagnosis and psychotherapeutic aspects of treatment for transsexuality, the majority do not cover surgery for sexual-reassignment. Yes, most insurers will cover the reconstruction of both male and female external sexual genitalia in cases of burn or accident. Yes, they pay for surgical rehabilitation for the intersex patient. They consider these surgeries "medically necessary."

Currently, many insurers classify transgender surgeries of all types as "experimental," even though many of the actual techniques and procedures used are identical to those used with burn, accident and intersex patients. I suspect that the underwriters are fearful that if they classify transgender surgery as a covered benefit, the floodgates will open, with thousands of transsexuals rushing to obtain surgery. I believe this assumption to be faulty in several respects:

- Is it rational to project that thousands of people are going to rush surgery departments to have their penises, vaginas and breasts excised? Any logical person should recognize that only a small percentage of the population wants to have their genitals removed and replaced.
- Second, if every transsexual approved for surgery were required to go through the steps I have outlined elsewhere in this book, only those who truly meet the criteria would be bankrolled for surgery.
- Third, I do believe there would be an initial sharp increase in surgeries as transsexuals who are saving up to pay for their surgery out-of-pocket come forward. After this one-time influx, however, I believe the actuaries and MBA's could easily calculate the expected numbers, and that the costs would not break the bank.

- Finally, while it is unfair and hypocritical for underwriters to disenfranchise this group, given the current state of health-care economics, I do not predict a major shift toward reimbursement. I hope I am wrong.

While it may sound bizarre, some transsexuals are "fortunate" enough to have medical problems that meet the insurer's criteria for a hysterectomy or mastectomy. In these cases, the individual is able to get at least a portion of the surgery paid for.

PART 5:
NUTS AND BOLTS

Will you describe and discuss transsexual surgery?

Yes, but with the following caveats. First, I am a clinical psychologist, not a physician or a surgeon. In discussions with my editor and publisher, we considered enlisting a team of qualified surgeons to write this section. We decided, finally, that the advantages of having the surgeries described by a medical layman in as close to everyday language as possible far outweighed the potential loss of technical precision. Medical language is so specialized that no book written for a larger public can adequately or accurately depict the complexities of the actual surgery.

The second issue involves the rapid emergence of new surgical and microsurgical techniques. It is my intention that this section provide the average reader with a general idea of what the various surgeries entail, and of some of the potential complications and negative outcomes reported in the medical literature. For the medically knowledgeable or curious reader, I have included references throughout this section; I encourage those who seek greater detail and precision of discussion to refer to the bibliography. A physician or surgeon should be consulted for information relevant to your particular situation or case.

The third and final caveat relates to value judgments. While I do so in other sections of the book, here I have attempted to refrain from making such judgments regarding specific surgical techniques, donor sites or particular surgery teams. In writing this section I ran a computer search of the topic spanning the last two years. While I cannot provide references to all transsexual surgery teams and techniques, I have strived to present a reasonable overview of the field as presented in the literature and in correspondence.

When discussing surgery, I will not soft peddle or talk around sensitive issues. Although transsexual surgery has been performed for several decades, it is still in many respects evolving. Imagine for a moment what is involved. The surgeons are going to cut, remove, mold, shape and remake a part of the human body. The individual's existing genitalia will be irreversibly altered, with absolutely no possibility of return to the original birth state. Plastic surgery and microsurgery will never be able to build a penis or a vagina that is as functional or cosmetically "perfect" as birth genitals.

Then there are the negative surgical realities: it will be expensive, painful, far less than "perfect," possibly unsuccessful and at worst life-threatening. While anesthesia is always risky, the risk is multiplied the longer one is under the knife, and the transsexual may be anesthetized for more than ten hours. I deliberately use tough words and expressions—e.g., "knife," "castration," "cutting it off" or "cutting it out"—because I want the transsexual to evaluate his or her ultimate decision with as much emotional clarity and awareness of exactly what takes place as possible. It should be emphasized that, as with many plastic surgery procedures, some follow-up surgeries will probably be necessary.

It should also be understood that, unlike non-transsexuals, transsexuals are not generally disturbed by raw descriptions of trauma to their birth genitals. While they may be concerned about surgical risks or complications, they have long dreamed and fantasized about having the surgery. The transsexual requires no coaxing or encouragement to undergo surgical reassignment. For many, it is the moment for which they have waited their entire lives.

The fields of genital reconstructive surgery and microsurgery in general are in a constant state of change and reevaluation, with each year bringing new innovations and better outcomes. I remember all too well the primitive surgeries of decades past, when the raw material for the neo-phallus consisted of stomach muscle grafts. In early stages of transformation the new penis was connected to the donor site in the abdomen, as well as to the pubic area. Once sufficient blood flow was realized, the neo-phallus was disconnected from the donor site. The graft was then freed and the tip of the newly constructed penis shaped by the surgeons.

These early "penises" were fraught with complications. They were not aesthetically pleasing, had no genital sensation, and were dysfunctional in most other respects. Today's neo-phallus is light years ahead of these early reconstructions. Surgery can create a neo-phallus that looks like a penis, through which urination can pass out of the bladder, and which possesses a degree of genital feeling. There is little question that tomorrow promises further enhancements, including perhaps the transplantation of genitals as we now transplant hearts and kidneys.

I encourage transsexuals to interview postoperative trans-sexuals, some of whom—if they are comfortable with you—may even allow you to view the outcome. Many will be willing to describe the pros and cons of various procedures.

Ask the surgeon for photos showing techniques and out-comes. Ask about complications. (No competent surgeon will underemphasize this important aspect of surgery.) Ask for references to people who have been through the exact type of operation he plans for you. Ask how long the team has been together, how many surgeries they have completed and how many they average each year. Ask if there have been any mor-talities or lawsuits. Do not be timid. If you are not comfortable with the answers, go somewhere else.

Check them out. And check them out. And check them out.

I tell everyone I work with to buy a bottle of a special per-fume and use it daily. The perfume is called Reasonable Expectations. If you fool yourself by denying the realities of medical science, you will be even more depressed when you are faced with new genitalia. Those who take the time to get their questions answered and accept the limitations of the surgery beforehand tend to fare better, gaining higher levels of per-sonal satisfaction.

Remember, the best references are those obtained from a satisfied customer. Some teams offer group therapy for pre- and post-surgical transsexuals; others host Clinic Days, when transsexuals from across the country come to be evaluated for inclusion in the program. Both of these afford excellent opportunities to obtain firsthand information from other transsexuals.

Readers who are interested in more detailed studies from a scientific or medical standpoint should refer to Appendixes C and D of this book. You can look up these studies in most university libraries. I recommend you talk with a librarian, who can assist you in a more detailed information search.

How do surgeons build a penis? What are some of the risks and complications?

There are a number of approaches to building a new penis. I use the world "build" because the penis must have mass, rigidity, genital feeling, shape and function. "Phalloplasty" is the surgical term for shaping or molding a new penis. There is no consensus on the best way to construct a neo-phallus. Every year new strategies are undertaken as old ones are modified, discarded or resurrected.

The hysterectomy is an obvious prerequisite for female-to-male transgender surgery. It is important that the hysterectomy be performed by a surgeon who is acquainted with transsexuality. This allows the hysterectomy to be accomplished in a way that prepares the individual's genital area for sexual reassignment.

A variety of muscles have been used as raw material for the penis. The tissues now most commonly used are from either the transsexual's forearm or calf muscle. Gilbert, Jordan, Devine and Winslow (1992) report using longitudinal and transverse rotations of forearm tissue to build the neo-phallus. This relatively thin, mostly hairless flap is richly vascularized (i.e., assured good blood flow), and has a nerve supply that is predictable anatomically and physiologically. With the newly constructed phallus, the patient retains erotic sensation, and is able to stand and urinate. A stiffener (to simulate erection) may be implanted at a later time.

The aforementioned team has carried out more than 50 microsurgical phalloplasties (Gilbert, 1995), and reports an increase in the number of female-to-male procedures as the quality of the outcome improves. Gottlieb and Levine (1993) also report equipping the forearm flap with a central neo-urethra. Sadove, Sengezer, McRoberts and Wells (1993) and a team of researchers prefer the fibula (calf) flap, stating that the radical forearm approach may result in a "floppy penis." One important factor, however, is the selection of a donor site with minimal hair growth; the arm flap is cited by several researchers as being ideal in this regard. There is still no universal agreement as to which donor site or technique is best.

I found no reports of neo-phallus construction in which the erection function resembled the actual function of a birth penis. In the birth penis the turgor, hardening and elevation of the phallus is the result of the erectile tissue filling with blood. However, the neo-phallus can be made functionally rigid using various internal or external aids. Unfortunately, a tendency on the part of rigid implants to erode and extrude (force out or dislocate) has been reported. Rigid implants may also be a source of embarrassment inasmuch as the new penis remains permanently erect. With hydraulic prosthetic implants, there is a high incidence of mechanical failure.

Successful intercourse without recourse to implants or aids has been reported by only a small number of female-to-male transsexuals.

A variety of problems have been reported with phalloplasty in general. In addition to common surgical risks, such as those related to anesthesia and infection, the transsexual is confronted with many others. The following listing is incomplete, but representative of potential complications:

- bladder spasms (Hage, de Graaf, van den Hoek and Bloem, 1993);
- meatal stenosis—a narrowing or stricture of a passageway, canal or opening (Ibid.);
- urinary incontinence (Fitzpatrick, Swierzewski and McGuire, 1993);
- colitis (Toolenaar, Freundt, Huikeshoven, Drogendijk, Jeekl and Chadha-Ajwani, 1993);
- fistulas, or abnormalities of the pipes, tubes or canals that connect two body organs or, in the case of urination, an internal body organ with the outside world (Hage, de Graaf, Bouman and Bloem, 1993);
- necrosis of the neo-phallus—in the extreme case, this results in the loss or literal death of the penis;

• scarring at the donor site. (Skilled surgery minimizes, but does not eliminate scarring.)

The glans, or mushroom-shaped tip of the penis, is generally regarded as essential from a visual perspective—and, properly constructed, may offer genital sensation. As a general rule, birth genital skin is preserved and integrated into the neo-phallus and related structures. Advances in microsurgery have greatly enhanced genital sensation and response. Some transsexuals report experiencing orgasms due to stimulation of their birth sex organs, which have been surgically integrated into their neo-penis.

Scrotal construction has utilized a technique whereby the labia majora (fleshy outer lips of the vagina) are expanded to build a scrotum. In scrotal construction, tissue expanders were inserted into the labia majora for several months prior to the construction of the neo-phallus. Sengezer and Sadove (1993) argue that the labia majora's location and skin tone makes it an excellent choice for use in creating a neo-scrotum. Hage, Bouman and Bloem (1993) of Amsterdam report the successful implantation of testicular prostheses in the labial skin neo-scrotum without prior tissue expansion.

Silicone implants may be used in various types of transgender surgery, including the shaping of the phallus and scrotum. Dr. Gilbert (1993) responds to the question of acquiring cancer from the surgical implantation of various biomedical inert silicone polymers. He notes there is no proven connection between the implants and cancer.

The functional ability to urinate through the neo-phallus is of major interest to nearly all female-to-male transsexuals. The anterior vaginal flap has been used (Hage, Torenbeek, Bouman and Bloem, 1993) to fashion a neo-urethra. Fistulas, strictures, urinary incontinence and urine residue are common complications with new urethral construction. The use of external devices for urination carry substantial risk of infection and trauma, and are aesthetically unsatisfactory to most transsexuals.

In terms of reproductive functioning, the newly built penis does not have the ejaculation response, nor do the newly constructed testicles and related structures manufacture semen. While the penis, testicles and scrotum may provide a powerful psychological boost to the transsexual, they are obviously not functional for reproduction. Privately, surgeons do discuss a vision of the future that includes transplantation of organs or portions thereof, although I suspect that the technical capability of transplantation will precede the actual use of such procedures by many years. Since mainstream society has so much trouble with sexuality in general, there will certainly be strong objections. Soliciting donors and obtaining family consent may also prove difficult.

In summary, surgery can offer the following:
• an aesthetically pleasing penis and glans, scrotum and testicles;
• reasonable function in terms of urination;
• reasonable function in terms of intercourse;
• genital sensation and, in some instances, orgasm.

As noted, there are complications and follow-up surgeries in most instances. Prosthetic aids or implants may be necessary. While the outcome will not be equivalent to birth genitals, it should be a reasonable facsimile.

Finally, a word on metadoioplasty or genitoplasty, a procedure that shapes an enlarged clitoris into a small "penis." One of the effects of the hormone testosterone is clitoral enlargement. This procedure, described by Gilbert (1995), was initially designed for patients who were unable or unwilling to go through phallic construction. The ventral chordee (the downward curvature of the vestigial penis) is released, to give the neo-phallus more length; the female urethra is directed forward and out to the clitoral tip; the pseudo-scrotum is sculpted from the labia majora.

Metadoioplasty does not require as long to perform as wholesale neo-phallus construction, and is generally less complicated with fewer risks and complications. The disadvantages of metadoioplasty, however, include a short penis which Gilbert (1995) likens to "a man just getting out of a cold shower," possible inability to urinate while standing, and possible inability to engage in sexual intercourse with the clitoral neo-penis.

While appropriate for older patients or those physically unable to undergo the lengthier phalloplasty procedures, most transsexuals opt for the more thorough phallic construction.

How do surgeons build a vagina?

"Vaginoplasty" refers to the surgical creation or reforming of tissue to build a new vagina. Crichton (1993) describes the results of 58 neo-vagina constructions, all of which entailed the use of peno-scroto-perineal flaps to line the newly built vagina, thus offering genital sensation. Selected tissues from the birth penis and scrotum are salvaged during the surgical castration, along with related nerves. These tissues are used to line the newly dissected vaginal canal. Intermittent use of a vibrator—versus an indwelling vaginal dilator—is recommended to keep the new vaginal passage clear and open.

Twenty-seven male-to-female transsexuals were studied by van Nort and Nicolai (1993). A "penile only" inversion method was used in eleven vaginal constructions. This involves the use of penile tissue only, inverted and tucked into the new vagina, lining the walls with genitally sensitive tissue and innervations. The doctors reported sixteen cases of vaginal construction using a combination of penile and scrotal skin flaps, once again inverting them into the newly constructed vaginal cavity. They reported greater vaginal width and superior subjective accounts with the penile-scrotal combination, but a better cosmetic result with the penile inversion only. Again, adequate dilation of the neo-vagina is essential for proper healing and long-term health.

S. O. Rubin (1993) reported in a Scandinavian journal the creation of a pseudoclitoris. The urethra and the glans penis were preserved in the castration. Subsequent surgery involved transposing and repositioning the sensitive, spongy tissue of the glans at the entrance of the newly constructed vagina, in essence preserving it as a pseudoclitoris. Rubin reports six successful outcomes. One possible danger involves insufficient circulation to the "blood sensitive" glans, which may result in necrosis, or literal death, of those sensitive tissues.

Similarly, Hage, Karim, Bloem, Suliman and van Alphen (1994) employed a free composite graft from the tip or head of the penile glans to create a clitoris-shaped structure ventral to the urethral orifice. Consistent with other researchers, they report the newly built "clitoris" to be functionally and aesthetically acceptable.

Drs. Freundt, Toolenaar, Jeekel, Drogendijk and Huikeshoven (1994) report three cases of prolapse—or collapse—of the neo-vagina, three or four years post-surgery. The problem was corrected using techniques too complex to describe here; again, the interested reader is referred to the original literature.

"Gender surgery should be considered as major surgery, with all the [attendant] complications: hemorrhage, infection, scarring...urethrocutaneous fistulae, urethral stenosis, pulmonary emboli, urinary infections and bowel infections" (Gilbert, 1995). Dr. Gilbert also cautions that while complication rates are low, it is important to inform the patient that surgical "touch ups" are generally required to achieve a maximal "functional aesthetic result." In summary, surgery can offer the following:

• aesthetically pleasing external genitalia;
• reasonable function in terms of urination;
• reasonable function in terms of sexual intercourse;
• genital sensation, including—in some instances—orgasm.

What was that about orgasm?

One of the major advances in genital construction has been the use of microsurgical techniques to enhance genital feeling. After years of experience and experimentation, surgeons have learned how to safeguard the necessary birth tissue, including nerve tissue, rearranging it to provide a pleasing sensory—as well as cosmetic—effect. Essential tissue from the birth genitals is salvaged during the early stages of surgery (hysterectomy in the case of the female-to-male, castration in the case of male-to-female). It is from these tissues, as well as from muscle tissue (described previously), that the new genitals are constructed.

Freundt, Toolenaar, Huikeshoven, Jeekel and Drogendijk (1993) used structured interviews and gynecological examinations to evaluate 19 male-to-female transsexuals with sigmoid vaginas. Sixteen reported having orgasms post-surgery, with twelve of those rating their sexual adjustment as "good" or "satisfactory."

Fourteen male-to-female transsexuals and nine female-to-male transsexuals were evaluated postoperatively for sexual satisfaction (Lief and Hubschman, 1993). General sexual satisfaction was reported in over 85 percent of the cases. The researchers concluded that sexual happiness is possible "despite inadequate sexual functioning."

Dr. Eldh (1993) studied 20 cases of male-to-female postoperative transsexuals in which the glans had been repositioned and formed into a clitoris. He reported "excellent sexual sensation of the clitoris" in 95 percent of the cases.

My only caution relates to the historical accuracy of patient self-report in the general literature. While I do not challenge specific self-report data, I must point out that only one study cited above included physical examinations as part of the evaluation. It is certainly conceivable that some of the "satisfaction" reported may derive from the functional role of being male or female in a sexual context, and not necessarily from any physiological orgasmic response.

What other feminizing or masculinizing surgical procedures are common?

For the male-to-female transsexual, a number of feminizing techniques are employed, including breast enlargement, nose surgery (rhinoplasty), liposuction, and ear-pinning (otoplasty). Procedures such as breast augmentation afford the surgeon additional challenges with the genetic male, who often presents with small nipples, chest hair and an inadequately delineated inframammary fold. Success in such cases may require a combination of strategies, including estrogen therapy and electrolysis for hair removal, as well as appropriate selection of an incision site and breast implant (Gilbert, 1995).

Surgical techniques to modify the facial skeleton (narrowing the nose, sculpting or shaving the jaw line, reducing the size of the eyebrows) and reshaping soft-tissue surgery can be effective in creating a poutier natural lip, narrowing and delineating the tip of the nose, and, with hair implantation, correcting male pattern baldness (Gilbert, 1995).

The principal challenge with the female-to-male transsexual is to disguise or remove obvious signs of being female, with the breasts presenting the most apparent problems. Success, as above, entails a combination of techniques, including breast reduction and sculpting the chest wall in a way to minimize scarring while preserving the nipples. Testosterone therapy cosmetically aids the outcome by providing hair growth and camouflage for conspicuous scars (Gilbert, 1995).

What are the positive and negative effects of hormone treatment?

In the most simplistic of terms, the birth male has male genitalia that produce the male hormone testosterone; the birth female has female genitalia that produce the female hormone estrogen. In order for the transsexual to approximate the hormonal makeup of the desired birth sex, hormone-replacement therapy is necessary.

Hormone-replacement therapy is prescribed for non-transsexual males and females who have had surgical or accidental removal of the sexual organs responsible for hormone production (testes in the birth male, ovaries in the birth female), or whose organs have ceased hormone production for one reason or another (e.g., menopause, dysfunction, disease).

Transsexuals have an added complicating factor: functioning sexual organs produce hormones that are in contradiction to their desired gender state. The male-to-female transsexual's testes may be producing testosterone as he is receiving estrogen-replacement therapy; the female-to-male transsexual's ovaries may be producing estrogen as she receives testosterone. Such complications are eliminated, of course, when surgical castration or hysterectomy is completed.

There are three positive effects of hormone therapy. The first involves suppression of undesired secondary sexual characteristics; the second, the enhancement of the desired secondary sexual characteristics; the third, the psychological effect of being "complete" in yet another way.

With the male-to-female transsexual, for example, hormone replacement may minimize male hair patterning (i.e., facial, head and body hair) while facilitating secondary feminine sexual characteristics (e.g., breast enlargement), resulting in the desired increased feminization of the individual. In a similar scenario, the female-to-male transsexual receiving hormone replacement wishes to maximize male hair patterning (beard growth, as well as arm, leg and chest hair) while minimizing feminine fat distribution patterning, resulting in the desired masculinization.

For information on specific drug formularies and dosages, I refer the reader to his or her physician.

Negative effects of hormone replacement are varied and may include the following problems:

- insulin resistance induced in healthy persons—by testosterone treatment in the case of females, by ethynyl estradiol treatment in the case of males (Polderman, Gooren, Asscheman, Bakker and Heine (1994);
- increased testosterone leading to increased adrenal gland response to ACTH (adrenocorticotropic hormone) (Polderman, Gooren and van der Veen (1994);
- long-term androgen treatment related to morphological change of the ectocervical epithelium, the portion of the cervix that protrudes into the vagina (Kwast, Dommerhold, van Vroonhoven and Chadha (1994);
- susceptibility to atherosclerotic cardiovascular disease (Polderman, Stehouwer, van Kamp, Dekker, Verheugt and Gooren, 1993).

It is important to note that individuals may request hormones for many reasons other than those relating to transsexuality. There are non-transsexuals, for example, who wish to have the secondary sexual characteristics of the opposite sex while maintaining and enjoying their own birth genitals.

A final note on hormones: it is essential that you receive your hormones from legitimate sources. Our physicians often find that individuals are taking sub-therapeutic doses, in other cases excessive amounts. While I am providing information from many fields, I urge you here, as elsewhere, to seek experienced professional help at all stages.

I am a transsexual, but I do not wish to undergo hormone treatment or surgical reassignment. Am I being reasonable?

It is important to point out that there are transsexuals who enter into a treatment or rehabilitation program, and those who choose not to. Most who enter a formal rehabilitation program choose to undertake hormone treatment. For many transsexuals, hormones represent a first practical step towards wholeness. It is therefore rare for a transsexual not to want to take hormones.

The answer is similar when discussing transgender surgical solutions. While more than 95 percent of those whom I have evaluated wish to have surgery, they probably wouldn't have come to see me if they weren't seriously considering it. There is a very small minority who are uncertain, and an even smaller group who tell me they do not wish to pursue the matter.

No one knows how many transsexuals never choose to enter a gender program. The number who silently suffer, or who treat themselves, may be substantial. I meet individuals every year who have suffered from this problem for decades before coming in for help or information. My best guess would be that there are hundreds of thousands of transsexuals who have never spoken to a professional.

I cannot estimate the number of transsexuals who do not enter a surgical reassignment program, but who nonetheless seek partial surgical resolutions to their gender dysphoria. No one can guess how many individuals have undergone facial, breast, neck, buttock and thigh enhancements and alterations to satisfy their transgender yearnings.

There is a substantial and developing body of literature concerning individuals who have attempted surgery on themselves. Fantasies of surgical self-intervention are not uncommon, and there have been more than a few instances where surgery has actually been attempted—with disastrous results.

What is the future of transsexual treatment?

Many professionals, including myself, postulate a non-environmental etiology (or course of development) for transsexuality. The apparent inability of the individual sufferer, or of medical and social science, to reverse these gender states clearly fuels the search for a chromosomal answer to transsexuality and other forms of gender disorder. Researcher-theorists such as Dr. John Money (see Foreword) foresee a day when science will provide us with genetic and/or developmental answers to this serious disability, offering a resolution before the "birth defect" blossoms—in other words, preventing or intervening before the faulty development occurs in the fetus or child.

From a surgical standpoint, the most ambitious possibility involves transplantation of actual genitalia, rather than construction of facsimiles from the host's own tissue. Surgeons privately admit that the technical possibility already exists. As discussed elsewhere, it is the political, theological and emotional reaction of the larger public that will likely stall development in this area. Plastic- and microsurgery will none the less continue to make tremendous advances.

In terms of psychotherapy and the social sciences, while I foresee incremental advances in theory and treatment, transsexuality has, in my view, crystallized in terms of general descriptive characteristics and overall development. While there will surely be additional information—especially, I hope, relating to the pre-adolescent years—I believe the next decade will be characterized by the wider acceptance of the transsexual phenomenon in America and elsewhere.

I also project major advances in the vast, if undefined, area of non-transsexual transgender problems. I believe the transgendered population to be many times larger than the transsexual group. Transsexuality may therefore rest at one end of a continuum of gender states, and I predict that this continuum will be studied and refined over the coming decade.

I predict also that the general public will have more difficulty accepting the larger transgendered community than it has had accepting transsexuals. The transgendered, non-transsexual condition, rightly or wrongly, will probably be perceived as having been determined by environmental-psychological variables rather than genetic ones. The public will view this group, as opposed to transsexuals proper, as having a good deal of "choice" in their ultimate gender presentation.

What is the Harry Benjamin society?

The Harry Benjamin International Gender Dysphoria Association, Inc., or HBIGDA, is a non-profit corporation that organizes conferences, encourages research, publishes newsletters and promulgates standards of care for the treatment of gender-dysphoric individuals. Their last international symposium was held September 7–10, 1995 in Bavaria, Germany.

Their current address is:

> P.O. Box 1718
> Sonoma, CA 95476
> Fax: (707) 938-2871

The HBIGDA's "Standards of Care" bulletin (1990 revision) is reprinted in its entirety in Appendix B.

Epilogue: Two Decades Later

Oh, how my world view has changed! I am writing this part eighteen years after my first contact with a transsexual. Two days ago, I attended the December gender clinic day with our team. The physicians, surgeons, therapists, nurses and staff were a pleasure to work with, as is always the case. The patients, a smaller group than usual, still hailed from across the country. Most arrived with a certain reluctance or trepidation—and a heart full of hope.

By mid-morning they had each completed several interviews and examinations, and were beginning to relax into the clinic environment. They retold their stories to us in private, and shared tidbits among themselves in the waiting room and at lunch. As the day ended, some left with their first prescription for hormones, some with surgery dates looming; others returned home to begin cross-dressing or therapy.

Having lived alone with their secret much of their lives, many had arrived with the sense that they had grown up misunderstood and that today would likely be no different. Most left believing that they were not alone, that they were indeed part of a community of transsexuals. Spending a day with people like themselves had enabled them to shed their fear of being the "only one," of being "special."

As I think back over nearly two decades, I ponder the many changes in perspective and attitude. More parents and mates accompany transsexuals on their journey than when I started out. Years ago, most of the transsexuals I evaluated were in the early stages of transformation, and we saw few, if any, female-to-males; today, nearly fifty percent of those at the clinic are female-to-male, ready or nearly ready for the final surgeries. In general, transsexuals come to us better informed, and their questions show a sophistication that was lacking twenty years ago. Their expectations post-surgery are closer to reality than in 1976.

I remember the words of Dr. Bill Groman, who taught a class in diagnostics at V.C.U. in Richmond: "Just because you understand why people are as they are, does not mean that they are healthy and normal."

I feel more and more affinity with this concept as time goes by, especially in relation to my work with and assessments of transsexuals. Although a diagnosis of transsexuality is the sine qua non for surgery, unless there is self-acceptance—unless the painful maturation and learning processes occur and until the new gender role becomes second nature—the individual will not be able to fully adapt.

The transsexual is a human being, reflecting all the positive and negative traits, all the biases and frailties that "normal folks" display. They are engineers, physicians, homeless people, psychologists, bricklayers, tug-boat captains, models, officers in the armed services, brokers, con artists, painters, farmers, teachers, television, radio and film celebrities, bakers, husbands and wives, sons and daughters of all colors, all ages, all sexes, all incomes and all religions. "Those people" are a reflection of ourselves: they are just as crazy as we are, just as loving as we are, and just as prejudiced in their own way as we are. Most Americans are unaware that they may know several transsexuals.

Yes, there are psychotic transsexuals. Yes, there are prostitutes who are transsexuals. Yes, there are transsexuals who are not very bright. There are, however, transsexuals who are decorated war heroes, elected officials in positions of high trust, philanthropists, intellectuals and financiers. Transsexuality is a regularly occurring phenomenon, spread across the face of mankind, in predictable patterns.

The following is a summary of my conjectures regarding the phenomenon called transsexuality:

1. The transsexual phenomenon is, minimally, a psychological birth defect. I project that genetic and brain researchers will ultimately find a biological basis for this phenomenon.

2. Because transsexuals have this apparent birth defect, they are not "normal." Fortunately, with current psychological, medical and surgical advances, they can be rehabilitated.

3. Transsexualism, regardless of its etiology or origin, results in a distortion of the individual's "body image," culminating in the rejection of biological birth gender.
4. Transsexualism thus predetermines the sufferer to a variety of emotional problems, such as depression and suicidal tendencies.
5. Like other biological defects, once gender dysphoria is medically or surgically corrected and the individual has dealt with the accompanying psychological damage and concomitant pain, the transsexual should be in a position to lead a "normal" life in most respects.
6. There remain a few areas in which the post-surgical transsexual cannot lead a "normal" life. These include the biological functions leading to and including pregnancy and childbirth. Transsexuals may, however, adopt children, utilize artificial insemination (depending on their partner's biological sex), surrogate mothering or any combination of the above as the means to having children and experiencing parenthood. The principal remaining areas in which the transsexual is not entirely "normal" relate to various hormonal and genital systems that medical science cannot fully duplicate. Most transsexuals who have completed psychotherapy are able to accept these limitations and lead a happy, productive life.
7. Transsexuals are found on every continent, within every race, country, age group and religion.
8. The phenomenon exists, in some instances, in the apparent absence of knowledge about other transsexuals. Transsexuals have come from small towns and remote villages where the media has not penetrated. Even where media exposure is a variable, it is unlikely that significant numbers of people seek to have their genitals excised based on media influence.
9. The transsexual population mirrors the general population in terms of sexual orientation. The largest number of transsexuals adopt a heterosexual orientation post-surgery. The second largest number of postoperative

transsexuals adopt a homosexual orientation. The rest—a very small number—are asexual or bisexual.

10. Aberrant personality variables—such as criminality, mental illness and mental retardation—occur in the transsexual as well as in the general population, and in proportionate numbers.

11. General intelligence testing and other measures of mental functioning will show similar results with transsexuals as with the general population. For example, if the average intelligence of the general population is 100, then the average intelligence of a transsexual would be 100; if one percent of the general population are geniuses, then one percent of transsexuals are geniuses.

I would further suggest that transsexuals do not "choose," in the traditional sense, to be transsexuals. Their biology and life experiences predispose them to this life path.

The following anecdote shows how medical science continues to miss the obvious. An older female-to-male transsexual candidate was asked why, at 61, she wanted to risk the lengthy (ten-hour) neo-phallic surgery. She replied: "For whatever reason, I was delivered into this world an incomplete soul. I have lived an incomplete life too long. I want to leave this life a complete man."

Those who still have doubts about the propriety of sex-reassignment surgery should take careful note of this reply, and of other transsexuals' relentless quest for wholeness.

APPENDIXES

Appendix A:
Gender Identity Disorders

GENDER IDENTITY DISORDER

(Reprinted with permission from the American Psychiatric Association: *Diagnostic and Statistical Manual of Mental Disorders*, Fourth Edition. Washington, D.C., American Psychiatric Association, 1994. pp. 532–538)

DIAGNOSTIC FEATURES

There are two components of Gender Identity Disorder, both of which must be present to make the diagnosis. There must be evidence of a strong and persistent cross-gender identification, which is the desire to be, or the insistence that one is, of the other sex (Criterion A). This cross-gender identification must not merely be a desire for any perceived cultural advantages of being the other sex. There must also be evidence of persistent discomfort about one's assigned sex or a sense of inappropriateness in the gender role of that sex (Criterion B). The diagnosis is not made if the individual has a concurrent physical intersex condition (e.g., androgen insensitivity syndrome or congenital adrenal hyperplasia) (Criterion C). To make the diagnosis, there must be evidence of clinically significant distress or impairment in social, occupational or other important areas of functioning (Criterion D).

In boys, the cross-gender identification is manifested by a marked preoccupation with traditionally feminine activities. They may have a preference for dressing in girls' or women's clothes or may improvise such items from available materials when genuine articles are unavailable. Towels, aprons and scarves are often used to represent long hair or skirts. There is a strong attraction for the stereotypical games and pastimes of girls. They particularly enjoy playing house, drawing pictures of beautiful girls and princesses, and watching television or videos of their favorite female characters. Stereotypical female-type dolls, such as Barbie, are often their favorite toys, and girls are their preferred playmates. When playing "house," these boys role-play female figures, most commonly "mother roles," and often are quite preoccupied with female fantasy figures. They avoid rough-and-tumble play and competitive sports and have little interest in cars and trucks or other nonaggressive but stereotypical boy's toys. They may express a wish to be a girl and assert that they will grow up to be a woman. They may insist on sitting to urinate and pretend not to have a penis by pushing it in between their legs. More rarely, boys with Gender Identity Disorder may state that they find their penis or testes disgusting, that they want to remove them, or that they have, or wish to have, a vagina.

Girls with Gender Identity Disorder display intense negative reactions to parental expectations or attempts to have them wear dresses or other feminine attire. Some may refuse to attend school or social events where such clothes may be required. They prefer boy's clothing and short hair, are often misidentified by strangers as boys, and may ask to be called by a boy's name. Their fantasy heroes are most often powerful male figures, such as Batman or Superman. These girls prefer boys as playmates, with whom they share interests in contact sports, rough-and-tumble play and traditional boyhood games. They show little interest in dolls or any form of feminine dress-up or role-play activity. A girl with this disorder may occasionally refuse to urinate in a sitting position. She may claim that she has or will grow a penis, and may not want to grow breasts or to menstruate. She may assert that she will grow up to be a man. Such girls typically reveal marked cross-gender identification in role-play, dreams and fantasies.

Adults with Gender Identity Disorder are preoccupied with a wish to live as a member of the other sex. This preoccupation may be manifested as an intense desire to adopt the social role of the other sex or to acquire the physical appearance of the other sex through hormonal or surgical manipulation. Adults with this disorder are uncomfortable being regarded by others as, or functioning in society as, a member of their designated sex. To varying degrees, they adopt the behavior, dress and mannerisms of the other sex. In private, these individuals may spend much time cross-dressed and working on the appearance of being the other sex. Many attempt to pass in public as the other sex. With cross-dressing and hormonal treatment (and for males, electrolysis), many individuals with this disorder may pass convincingly as the other sex. The sexual activity of these individuals with same-sex partners is generally constrained by the preference that their partners neither see nor touch their genitals. For some males who present later in life (often following marriage), sexual activity with a woman is accompanied by the fantasy of being lesbian lovers, or that his partner is a man and he is a woman.

In adolescents, the clinical features may resemble either those of children or those of adults, depending on the individual's developmental level, and the criteria should be applied accordingly. In a younger adolescent, it may be more difficult to arrive at an accurate diagnosis because of the adolescent's guardedness. This may be increased if the adolescent feels ambivalent about cross-gender identification or feels that it is unacceptable to the family. The adolescent may be referred because the parents or teachers are concerned about social isolation or peer teasing and rejection. In such circumstances, the diagnosis should be reserved for those adolescents who appear quite cross-gender identified in their dress and who engage in behaviors that suggest significant cross-gender identification (e.g., shaving legs in males). Clarifying the diagnosis in children and adolescents may require monitoring over an extended period of time.

Distress or disability in individuals with Gender Identity Disorder is manifested differently across the life cycle. In young children, distress is manifested by the stated unhappiness about their assigned sex. Preoccupation with cross-gender wishes often interferes with ordinary activities. In older children, failure to develop age-appropriate same-sex peer relationships and skills often leads to isolation and distress, and some children may refuse to attend school because of teasing or pressure to dress in attire stereotypical of their assigned sex. In adolescents and adults, preoccupation with cross-gender wishes often interferes with ordinary activities. Relationship difficulties are common, and functioning at school or at work may be impaired.

SPECIFIERS

For sexually mature individuals, the following specifiers may be noted based on the individuals' sexual orientation: "Sexually Attracted to Males," "Sexually Attracted to Females," "Sexually Attracted to Both," and "Sexually Attracted to Neither." Males with Gender Identity Disorder include substantial proportions with all four specifiers. Virtually all females with Gender Identity Disorder will receive the same specifier—"Sexually Attracted to Females"—although there are exceptional cases involving females who are "Sexually Attracted to Males."

Recording Procedures The assigned diagnostic code depends on the individual's current age: if the disorder occurs in childhood, the code 302.6 is used; for an adolescent or adult, 302.85 is used.

ASSOCIATED FEATURES AND DISORDERS

Associated descriptive features and mental disorders. Many individuals with Gender Identity Disorder become socially isolated. Isolation and ostracism contribute to low self-esteem and may lead to school aversion or dropping out of school. Peer ostracism and teasing are especially common sequelae for boys with the disorder. Boys with Gender Identity Disorder often show marked feminine mannerisms and speech patterns.

The disturbance can be so pervasive that the mental lives of some individuals revolve only around those activities that lessen gender distress. They are often preoccupied with appearance, especially early in the transition to living in the opposite sex role. Relationships with one or both parents also may be seriously impaired. Some males with Gender Identity Disorder resort to self-treatment with hormones and may very rarely perform their own castration or penectomy. Especially in urban centers, some males with the disorder may engage in prostitution, which places them at high risk for human immunodeficiency virus (HIV) infection. Suicide attempts and Substance-Related Disorders are commonly associated.

Children with Gender Identity Disorder may manifest coexisting Separation Anxiety Disorder, Generalized Anxiety

Disorder, and symptoms of depression. Adolescents are particularly at risk for depression, and suicidal ideation and suicide attempts. In adults, anxiety and depressive symptoms may be present. Some adult males have a history of Transvestic Fetishism, as well as other Paraphilias. Associated Personality Disorders are more common among males than among females being evaluated at adult gender clinics.

Associated laboratory findings. There is no diagnostic test specific for Gender Identity Disorder. In the presence of a normal physical examination, karyotyping for sex chromosomes and sex-hormone assays are usually not indicated. Psychological testing may reveal cross-gender identification or behavior patterns.

Associated physical examination findings and general medical conditions. Individuals with Gender Identity Disorder have normal genitalia (in contrast to the ambiguous genitalia or hypogonadism found in physical intersex conditions). Adolescents and adult males with Gender Identity Disorder may show breast enlargement resulting from hormone ingestion, hair denuding from temporary or permanent depilation, and other physical changes as a result of procedures such as rhinoplasty or thyroid cartilage shaving (surgical reduction of the Adam's apple). Distorted breasts or breast rashes may be seen in females who wear breast binders. Postsurgical complications in genetic females include prominent chest-wall scars, and in genetic males, vaginal strictures, rectovaginal fistulas, urethral stenoses and misdirected urinary streams. Adult females with Gender Identity Disorder may have a higher than expected likelihood of polycystic ovarian disease.

SPECIFIC AGE AND GENDER FEATURE

Females with Gender Identity Disorders generally experience less ostracism because of cross-gender interests and may suffer less from peer rejection, at least until adolescence. In child clinic samples, there are approximately five boys for each girl referred with this disorder. In adult clinic samples, men outnumber women by about two or three times. In children, the referral bias toward males may partly reflect the greater stigma that cross-gender behavior carries for boys than for girls.

PREVALENCE

There are no recent epidemiological studies to provide data on prevalence of Gender Identity Disorder. Data from smaller countries in Europe with access to total population statistics and referrals suggest that roughly 1 per 30,000 adult males and 1 per 100,000 adult females seek sex-reassignment surgery.

COURSE

For clinically referred children, onset of cross-gender interests and activities is usually between ages 2 and 4 years, and some parents report that their child has always had cross-gender interests. Only a very small number of children with Gender Identity Disorder will continue to have symptoms that meet criteria for Gender Identity Disorder in later adolescence or adulthood. Typically, children are referred around the time of school entry because of parental concern that what they regarded as a "phase" does not appear to be passing. Most children with Gender Identity Disorder display less overt cross-gender behaviors with time, parental intervention, or response from peers. By late adolescence or adulthood, about three-quarters of boys who had a childhood history of Gender Identity Disorder report a homosexual or bisexual orientation, but without concurrent Gender Identity Disorder. Most of the remainder report a heterosexual orientation, also without concurrent Gender Identity Disorder. The corresponding percentages for sexual orientation in girls are not known. Some adolescents may develop a clearer cross-gender identification and request sex-reassignment surgery, or may continue in a chronic course of gender confusion or dysphoria.

In adult males, there are two different courses for the development of Gender Identity Disorder. The first is a continuation of Gender Identity Disorder that had an onset in childhood or early adolescence. These individuals typically present in late adolescence or adulthood. In the other course, the more overt signs of cross-gender identification appear later and more gradually, with a clinical presentation in early to mid-adulthood usually following, but sometimes concurrent with, Transvestic Fetishism. The later-onset group may be more fluctuating in the degree of cross-gender identification, more ambivalent about sex-reassignment surgery, more likely to be sexually attracted to women, and less likely to be satisfied after sex-reassignment surgery. Males with Gender Identity Disorder who are sexually attracted to males tend to present in adolescence or early adulthood with a lifelong history of gender dysphoria. In contrast, those who are sexually attracted to females, to both males and females, or to neither sex tend to present later and typically have a history of Transvestic Fetishism. If Gender Identity Disorder is present in adulthood, it tends to have a chronic course, but spontaneous remission has been reported.

Differential Diagnosis

Gender Identity Disorder can be distinguished from simple *nonconformity to stereotypical sex role behavior* by the extent and pervasiveness of the cross-gender wishes, interests, and activities. This disorder is not meant to describe a child's nonconformity to stereotypic sex-role behavior as, for example, in "tomboyishness" in girls or "sissyish" behavior in boys. Rather, it represents a profound disturbance of the individual's sense of identity with regard to maleness or femaleness. Behavior in children that merely does not fit the cultural stereotype of masculinity or femininity should not be given the diagnosis unless the full syndrome is present, including marked distress or impairment.

Transvestic Fetishism occurs in heterosexual (or bisexual) men for whom the cross-dressing behavior is for the purpose of sexual excitement. Aside from cross-dressing, most individuals with Transvestic Fetishism do not have a history of childhood cross-gender behaviors. Males with a presentation that meets full criteria for Gender Identity Disorder as well as Transvestic Fetishism should be given both diagnoses. If gender dysphoria is present in an individual with Transvestic Fetishism but full criteria for Gender Identity Disorder are not met, the specifier "With Gender Dysphoria" can be used.

The category *Gender Identity Disorder Not Otherwise Specified* can be used for individuals who have a gender identity problem with a *concurrent congenital intersex condition* (e.g., androgen insensitivity syndrome or congenital adrenal hyperplasia).

In *Schizophrenia,* there may rarely be delusions of belonging to the other sex. Insistence by a person with a Gender Identity Disorder that he or she is of the other sex is not considered a delusion, because what is invariably meant is that the person feels like a member of the other sex rather than truly believes that he or she is a member of the other sex. In very rare cases, however, Schizophrenia and severe Gender Identity Disorder may coexist.

DIAGNOSTIC CRITERIA FOR GENDER IDENTITY DISORDER

A. A strong and persistent cross-gender identification (not merely a desire for any perceived cultural advantages of being the other sex).

   In children, the disturbance is manifested by four (or more) of the following:
   1. repeatedly stated desire to be, or insistence that he or she is, the other sex
   2. in boys, preference for cross-dressing or simulating female attire; in girls, insistence on wearing only stereotypical masculine clothing
   3. strong and persistent preferences for cross-sex roles in make-believe play or persistent fantasies of being the other sex
   4. intense desire to participate in the stereotypical games and pastimes of the other sex
   5. strong preference for playmates of the other sex

   In adolescents and adults, the disturbance is manifested by symptoms such as a stated desire to be the other sex, frequent passing as the other sex, desire to live or be treated as the other sex, or the conviction that he or she has the typical feelings and reactions of the other sex.

B. Persistent discomfort with his or her sex or sense of inappropriateness in the gender role of that sex.

   In children, the disturbance is manifested by any of the following: in boys, assertion that his penis or testes are disgusting or will disappear, or assertion that it would be better not to have a penis, or aversion toward rough-and-tumble play and rejection of male stereotypical toys, games and activities; in girls, rejection of urinating in a sitting position, assertion that she has or will grow a penis, or assertion that she does not want to grow breasts or menstruate, or marked aversion toward normative feminine clothing.

In adolescents and adults, the disturbance is manifested by symptoms such as preoccupation with getting rid of primary and secondary sex characteristics (e.g., request for hormones, surgery or other procedures to physically alter sexual characteristics to simulate the other sex) or belief that he or she was born the wrong sex.

C. The disturbance is not concurrent with a physical intersex condition.

D. The disturbance causes clinically significant distress or impairment in social, occupational or other important areas of functioning.

Appendix B:
Standards of Care

THE HORMONAL AND SURGICAL SEX REASSIGNMENT OF
GENDER DYSPHORIC PERSONS
Original draft prepared by the founding committee of the Harry
Benjamin International Gender Dysphoria Association, Inc.

Paul A. Walker, Ph.D. (Chairperson)
Jack C. Berger, M.D.
Richard Green, M.D.
Donald R. Laub, M.D.
Charles L. Reynolds, M.D.
Leo Wollman, M.D.

Revised draft (1/90) approved by: The majority of the
membership of the Harry Benjamin International Gender
Dysphoria Association, Inc. (1/90)
[1990 revisions appear in brackets.]

1. INTRODUCTION

As of the beginning of 1979, an undocumentable estimate of
the number of adult Americans hormonally and surgically sex-
reassigned ranged from 3,000 to 6,000. Also undocumentable
is the estimate that between 30,000 and 60,000 U.S.A. citizens
consider themselves to be valid candidates for sex reassignment. World estimates are not available. As of mid-1978,
approximately 40 centers in the Western hemisphere offered
surgical sex reassignment to persons having a multiplicity of
behavioral diagnoses applied under a multiplicity of criteria.

In recent decades, the demand for sex reassignment has
increased as have the number and variety of possible psychologic, hormonal and surgical treatments. The rationale upon
which such treatments are offered have become more and
more complex. Varied philosophies of appropriate care have
been suggested by various professionals identified as experts
on the topic of gender identity. However, until the present, no
statement of the standard of care to be offered to gender

dysphoric patients (sex reassignment applicants) has received official sanction by any identifiable professional group. The present document is designed to fill that void.

2. STATEMENT OF PURPOSE

Harry Benjamin International Gender Dysphoria Association, Inc., presents the following as its explicit statement on the appropriate standards of care to be offered to applicants for hormonal and surgical sex reassignment.

3. DEFINITIONS

3.1 Standard of care

The standards of care, as listed below, are *minimal* requirements and are not to be construed as optimal standards of care. It is recommended that professionals involved in the management of sex reassignment cases use the following as *minimal* criteria for the evaluation of their work. It should be noted that some experts on gender identity recommend that the time parameters listed below should be doubled, or tripled. It is recommended that the reasons for any exceptions to these standards, in the management of any individual case, be very carefully documented. Professional opinions differ regarding the permissibility of, and the circumstances warranting, any such exception.

3.2 Hormonal sex reassignment

Hormonal sex reassignment refers to the administration of androgens to genotypic and phenotypic females, and the administration of estrogens and/or progesterones to geno-typic and phenotypic males, for the purpose of effecting so-matic changes in order for the patient to more closely approximate the physical appearance of the genotypically other sex. Hormonal sex reassignment does not refer to the administration of hormones for the purpose of medical care and/or research conducted for the treatment or study of non-gender dysphoric medical condition (e.g., aplastic anemia, impotence, cancer, etc.).

3.3 Surgical sex reassignment

Genital surgical sex reassignment refers to surgery of the genitalia and/or breasts performed for the purpose of altering the morphology in order to approximate the physical appearance of the genetically-other sex in persons diagnosed as gender dysphoric. Such surgical procedures as mastectomy, reduction mammoplasty, augmentation mammoplasty, castration, orchidectomy, penectomy, vaginoplasty, hysterectomy, salpingectomy, vaginectomy, oophorectomy and phalloplasty—in the absence of any diagnosable birth defect or other medically defined pathology, except gender dysphoria, are included in this category labeled surgical sex reassignment.

Non-genital surgical sex reassignment refers to any and all other surgical procedures of non-genital, or non-breast sites (nose, throat, chin, cheeks, hips, etc.) conducted for the purpose of effecting a more masculine appearance in a genetic female or for the purpose of effecting a more feminine appearance in a genetic male, in the absence of identifiable pathology which would warrant such surgery regardless of the patient's genetic sex (facial injuries, hermaphroditism, etc.).

3.4 Gender Dysphoria

Gender Dysphoria herein refers to that psychological state whereby a person demonstrates dissatisfaction with their sex of birth and the sex role, as socially defined, which applies to that sex, and who requests hormonal and surgical sex reassignment.

3.5 Clinical behavioral scientist

Possession of an academic degree in a behavioral science does not necessarily attest to the possession of sufficient training or competence to conduct psychotherapy, psychologic counseling, nor diagnosis of gender identity problems. Persons recommending sex reassignment surgery or hormone therapy should have documented training and experience in the diagnosis and treatment of a broad range of psychologic conditions. Licensure or certification as a psychological therapist or counselor does not necessarily attest to competence in sex therapy. Persons recommending sex reassignment surgery or hormone therapy should have the documented training and experience to diagnose and treat a broad range of sexual conditions. Certification in sex therapy or counseling does not necessarily attest to competence in the diagnosis and treatment of gender identity conditions or disorders. Persons recommending sex reassignment surgery or hormone therapy should have proven competence in general psychotherapy, sex therapy, and gender counseling/therapy.

Any and all recommendations for sex reassignment surgery and hormone therapy should be made only by clinical behavioral scientists possessing the following minimal documentable credentials and expertise:

3.5.1. A minimum of a Masters Degree in a clinical behavioral science, granted by an institution of education accredited by a national or regional accrediting board.

3.5.2. One recommendation, of the two required for sex reassignment surgery, must be made by a person possessing a doctoral degree (e.g., Ph.D., Ed.D., D.Sc., D.S.W., Psy.D., or M.D.) in a clinical behavioral science, granted by an institution of education accredited by a national or regional accrediting board.

3.5.3. Demonstrated competence in psychotherapy as indicated by a license to practice medicine, psychology, clinical social work, marriage and family counseling, or social psychotherapy, etc., granted by the state of residence. In states where no such appropriate license board exists, persons recommending sex reassignment surgery or hormone therapy should have been certified by a nationally known and reputable association, based on education and experience criteria, and, preferably, some form of testing (and not simply on membership received for dues paid) as an accredited or certified therapist/counselor (e.g. American Board of Psychiatry and Neurology, Diplomate in Psychology from the American Board of Professional Psychologists, Certified Clinical Social Workers, American Association of Marriage and Family Therapists, American Professional Guidance Association, etc.).

3.5.4. Demonstrated specialized competence in sex therapy and theory as indicated by documentable training and supervised clinical experience in sex therapy (in some states professional licensure requires training in human sexuality; also, persons should have approximately the training and experience as required for certification as a Sex Therapist or Sex Counselor by the American Association of Sex Educators, Counselors and Therapists, or as required for membership in the Society for Sex Therapy and Research). Continuing education in human sexuality and sex therapy should also be demonstrable.

3.5.5. Demonstrated and specialized competence in therapy, counseling, and diagnosis of gender identity disorders as documentable by training and supervised clinical experience, along with continuing education.

The behavioral scientists recommending sex reassignment surgery and hormone therapy and the physician and surgeon(s) who accept those recommendations share responsibility for certifying that the recommendations are made based on competency indicators as described above.

4. PRINCIPLES AND STANDARDS

Introduction

4.1.1. Principle 1. Hormonal and surgical sex reassignment is extensive in its effects, is invasive to the integrity of the human body, has effects and consequences which are not, or are not readily, reversible, and may be requested by persons experiencing short-termed delusions or beliefs which may later be changed and reversed.

4.1.2. Principle 2. Hormonal and surgical sex reassignment are procedures requiring justification and are not of such minor consequence as to be performed on an elective basis.

4.1.3. Principle 3. Published and unpublished case histories are known in which the decision to undergo hormonal and surgical sex reassignment was, after the fact, regretted and the final result of such procedures proved to be psychologically debilitating to the patients.

4.1.4. Standard 1. Hormonal and/or surgical sex reassignment on demand (i.e., justified simply because the patient has requested such procedures) is contraindicated. It is herein declared to be professionally improper to conduct, offer, administer or perform hormonal sex reassignment and/or surgical sex reassignment without careful evaluation of the patient's reasons for requesting such services and evaluation of the beliefs and attitudes upon which such reasons are based. [*The present standards provide no guidelines for the granting of non-genital/breast cosmetic or reconstructive surgery. The decision to perform such surgery is left to the patient and surgeon. The original draft of this document did recommend the following however (rescinded 1/80): "Non-genital sex reassignment (facial, hip, limb, etc.) shall be preceded by a period of at least six months during which time the patient lives full-time in the social role of the genetically other sex."*]

4.2.1. Principle 4. The analysis or evaluation of reasons, motives, attitudes, purposes, etc., requires skills not usually associated with the professional training of persons other than clinical behavioral scientists.

4.2.2. Principle 5. Hormonal and/or surgical sex reassignment is performed for the purpose of improving the quality of life as subsequently experienced and such experiences are most properly studied and evaluated by the clinical behavioral scientist.

4.2.3. Principle 6. Hormonal and surgical sex reassignment are usually offered to persons, in part, because a psychiatric/psychologic diagnosis of transsexualism [see Appendix A], or some related diagnosis, has been made. Such diagnoses are properly made only by clinical behavioral scientists.

4.2.4. Principle 7. Clinical behavioral scientists, in deciding to make the recommendation in favor of hormonal and/or surgical sex reassignment share the moral responsibility for that decision with the physician and/or surgeon who accepts the recommendation.

4.2.5. Standard 2. Hormonal and surgical (genital and breast) sex reassignment must be preceded by a firm written recommendation for such procedures made by a clinical behavioral scientist who can justify making such a recommendation by appeal to training or professional experience in dealing with sexual disorders, especially the disorders of gender identity and role.

4.3.1. Principle 8. The clinical behavioral scientist's recommendation for hormonal and/or surgical sex reassignment should, in part, be based upon an evaluation of how well the patient fits the diagnostic criteria for transsexualism as listed in the DSM-III-R category 302.50 to wit:

"A. Persistent discomfort and sense of inappropriateness about one's assigned sex.

B. Persistent preoccupation for at least two years with getting rid of one's primary and secondary sex characteristics and acquiring the sex characteristics of the other sex.

C. The person has reached puberty."

This definition of transsexualism is herein interpreted not to exclude persons who meet the above criteria but who otherwise may, on the basis of their past behavioral histories, be conceptualized and classified as transvestites and/or effeminate male homosexuals or masculine female homosexuals.

4.3.2. Principle 9. The intersexed patient (with a documented hormonal or genetic abnormality) should first be treated by procedures commonly accepted as appropriate for such medical conditions.

4.3.3. Principle 10. The patient having a psychiatric diagnosis (i.e., schizophrenia) in addition to a diagnosis of transsexualism should first be treated by procedures commonly accepted as appropriate for such non-transsexual psychiatric diagnoses.

4.3.4. Standard 3. Hormonal and surgical sex reassignment may be made available to intersexed patients and to patients having non-transsexual psychiatric/psychologic diagnoses if the patient and therapist have fulfilled the requirements of the herein listed standards; if the patient can be reasonably expected to be habilitated or rehabilitated, in part, by such hormonal and surgical sex reassignment procedures; and if all other commonly accepted therapeutic approaches to such intersexed or non-transsexual/psychiatrically/psychologically diagnosed patients have been either attempted, or considered for use prior to the decision not to use such alternative therapies. The diagnosis of schizophrenia, therefore, does not necessarily preclude surgical and hormonal sex reassignment.

Hormonal Sex Reassignment

4.4. Principle 11. Hormonal sex reassignment is both therapeutic and diagnostic in that the patient requesting such therapy either reports satisfaction or dissatisfaction regarding the results of such surgery.

4.4.2. Principle 12. Hormonal sex reassignment may have some irreversible effects (infertility, hair growth, voice deepening and clitoral enlargement in the female-to-male patient and infertility and breast growth in the male-to-female patient) and, therefore, such therapy must be offered only under the guidelines proposed in the present standards.

4.4.3. Principle 13. Hormonal sex reassignment should precede surgical sex reassignment as its effects (Patient satisfaction or dissatisfaction) may indicate or contraindicate later surgical sex reassignment.

4.4.4. Standard 4. The initiation of hormonal sex reassignment shall be preceded by recommendation for such hormonal therapy, made by a clinical behavioral scientist. [*This standard, in the original draft, recommended that the patient must have lived successfully in the social/gender role of the genetically other sex for at least three months prior to the initiation of hormonal sex reassignment. This requirement was rescinded 1/80.*]

4.5.1. Principle 14. The administration of androgens to females and of estrogens and/or progesterones to males may lead to mild or serious health-threatening complications.

4.5.2. Principle 15. Persons who are in poor health, or who have identifiable abnormalities in blood chemistry, may be at above average risk to develop complications should they receive hormonal medication.

4.5.3. Standard 5. The physician prescribing hormonal medication to a person for the purpose of effecting hormonal sex reassignment must warn the patient of possible negative complications which may arise and that physician should also make available to the patient (or refer the patient to a facility offering) monitoring of relevant blood chemistries and routine physical examinations including, but not limited to, the measurement of SGPT in persons receiving testosterone and the measurement of SGPT, bilirubin, triglycerides and fasting glucose in persons receiving estrogens.

4.6.1. Principle 16. The diagnostic evidence for transsexualism (see *4.3.1.* above) requires that the clinical behavioral scientist have knowledge, independent of the patient's verbal claim, that the dysphoria, discomfort, sense of inappropriateness and wish to be rid of one's own genitals, have existed for at least two years. This evidence may be obtained by interview of the patient's appointed informant (friend or relative) or it may best be obtained by the fact that the clinical behavioral scientist has professionally known the patient for an extended period of time.

4.6.2. Standard 6. The clinical behavioral scientist making the recommendation in favor of hormonal sex reassignment shall have known the patient in a psychotherapeutic relationship for at least three months prior to making said recommendation.

Surgical (Genital and/or Breast) Sex Reassignment

4.7.1. Principle 17. Peer review is a commonly accepted procedure in most branches of science and is used primarily to ensure maximal efficiency and correctness of scientific decisions and procedures.

4.7.2. Principle 18. Clinical behavioral scientists must often rely on possibly unreliable or invalid sources of information (patients' verbal reports or the verbal reports of the patients' families and friends) in making clinical decisions and in judging whether or not a patient has fulfilled the requirements of the herein listed standards.

4.7.3. Principle 19. Clinical behavioral scientists given the burden of deciding who to recommend for hormonal and surgical sex reassignment and for whom to refuse such recommendations are subject to extreme social pressure and possible manipulation as to create an atmosphere in which charges of laxity, favoritism, sexism, financial gain, etc., may be made.

4.7.4. Principle 20. A plethora of theories exist regarding the etiology of gender dysphoria and the purposes or goals of hormonal and/or surgical sex reassignment such that the clinical behavioral scientist making the decision to recommend such reassignment for a patient does not enjoy the comfort or security of knowing that his or her decision would be supported by the majority of his or her peers.

4.7.5. Standard 7. The clinical behavioral scientist recommending that a patient applicant receive surgical (genital and breast) sex reassignment must obtain peer review, in the format of a clinical behavioral scientist peer who will personally examine the patient applicant, on at least one occasion, and who will, in writing, state that he or she concurs with the decision of the original clinical behavioral scientist. Peer review (a second opinion) is not required for hormonal sex reassignment. Nongenital/breast surgical sex reassignment does not require the recommendation of a behavioral scientist. At least one of the two behavioral scientists making the favorable recommendation for surgical (genital and breast) sex reassignment must be a doctoral level behavioral scientist. [*In the original and 1/80 version of these standards, one of the clinical behavioral scientists was required to be a psychiatrist. That requirement was rescinded in 3/81.*]

4.8.1. Standard 8. The clinical behavioral scientist making the primary recommendation in favor of genital (surgical) sex reassignment shall have known the patient in a psychotherapeutic relationship for at least six months prior to making said recommendation. That clinical behavioral scientist should have access to the results of psychometric testing (including IQ testing of the patient) when such testing is clinically indicated.

4.9.1. Standard 9. Genital sex reassignment shall be preceded by a period of at least 12 months during which time the patient lives full-time in the social role of the genetically other sex.

4.10.1. Principle 21. Genital surgical sex reassignment includes the invasion of, and the alteration of, the genitourinary tract. Undiagnosed pre-existing genitourinary disorders may complicate later genital surgical sex reassignment.

4.10.2. Standard 10. Prior to genital surgical sex reassignment a urological examination should be conducted for the purpose of identifying and perhaps treating abnormalities of the genitourinary tract. [*This requirement was rescinded 1/90.*]

4.11.1. Standard 11. The physician administering or performing surgical (genital) sex reassignment is guilty of professional misconduct if he or she does not receive written recommendations in favor of such procedures from at least two clinical behavioral scientists; at least one of which is a doctoral level clinical behavioral scientist and one of whom has known the patient in a professional relationship for at least six months.

Miscellaneous

4.12.1. Principle 22. The care and treatment of sex reassignment applicants or patients often causes special problems for the professionals offering such care and treatment. These special problems include, but are not limited to, the need for the professional to cooperate with education of the public to justify his or her work, the need to document the case history perhaps more completely than is customary in general patient care, the need to respond to multiple, nonpaying, service applicants and the need to be receptive and responsive to the extra demands for services and assistance often made by sex reassignment applicants as compared to other patient groups.

4.12.2. Principle 23. Sex reassignment applicants often have need for post-therapy (psychologic, hormonal and surgical) follow-up care for which they are unable or unwilling to pay.

4.12.3. Principle 24. Sex reassignment applicants often are in a financial status which does not permit them to pay excessive professional fees.

4.12.4. Standard 12. It is unethical for professionals to charge sex reassignment applicants "whatever the traffic will bear" or excessive fees far beyond the normal fees charged for similar services by the professional. It is permissible to charge sex reassignment applicants for services in advance of the tendering of such services even if such an advance fee arrangement is not typical of the professional's practice. It is permissible to charge patients, in advance, for expected services such as post-therapy follow-up care and/or counseling. It is unethical to charge patients for services which are essentially research and which services do not directly benefit the patient.

4.13.1. Principle 25. Sex reassignment applicants often experience social, legal and financial discrimination not known, at present, to be prohibited by federal or state law.

4.13.2. Principle 26. Sex reassignment applicants often must conduct formal or semiformal legal proceedings (i.e., in-court appearances against insurance companies or in pursuit of having legal documents changed to reflect their new sexual and genderal status, etc.).

4.13.3. Principle 27. Sex reassignment applicants, in pursuit of what are assumed to be their civil rights as citizens, are often in need of assistance in the form of copies of records, letters of endorsement, court testimony, etc. from the professionals involved in their case.

4.13.4. Standard 13. It is permissible for a professional to charge only the normal fee for services needed by a patient in pursuit of his or her civil rights. Fees should not be charged for services for which, for other patient groups, such fees are not normally charged.

4.14.1. Principle 28. Hormonal and surgical sex reassignment has been demonstrated to be a rehabilitative, or habilitative, experience for properly selected adult patients.

4.14.2. Principle 29. Hormonal and surgical sex reassignment are procedures which must be requested by, and performed only with the agreement of, the patient having informed consent. Sex reannouncement or sex reassignment procedures conducted on infantile or early childhood intersexed patients are common medical practices and are not included in or affected by the present discussion.

4.14.3. Principle 30. Sex reassignment applicants often, in their pursuit of sex reassignment, believe that hormonal and surgical sex reassignment have fewer risks than such procedures are known to have.

4.14.4. Standard 14. Hormonal and surgical sex reassignment may be conducted or administered only to persons obtaining their legal majority (as defined by state law) or to persons declared by the courts as legal adults (emancipated minors).

4.15.1. Standard 15. Hormonal and surgical sex reassignment may be conducted or administered only after the patient applicant has received full and complete explanations, preferably in writing, in words understood by the patient applicant, of all risks inherent in the requested procedures.

4.16.1. Principle 31. Gender dysphoric sex reassignment applicants and patients enjoy the same rights to medical privacy as does any other patient group.

4.16.2. Standard 16. The privacy of the medical record of the sex reassignment patient shall be safeguarded according to procedures in use to safeguard the privacy of any other patient group.

5. EXPLICATION

5.1. Prior to the initiation of hormonal sex reassignment:

5.1.1. The patient must demonstrate that the sense of discomfort with the self and the urge to rid the self of the genitalia and the wish to live in the genetically other sex role have existed for at least two years.

5.1.2. The patient must be known to a clinical behavioral scientist for at least three months and that clinical behavioral scientist must endorse the patient's request for hormone therapy.

5.1.3. Prospective patients should receive a complete physical examination which includes, but is not limited to, the measurement of SGPT in persons to receive testosterone and the measurement of SGPT, bilirubin, triglycerides and fasting glucose in persons to receive estrogens.

5.2. Prior to the initiation of genital or breast sex reassignment (Penectomy, orchidectomy, castration, vaginoplasty, mastectomy, hysterectomy, oophorectomy, salpingectomy, vaginectomy, phalloplasty, reduction mammoplasty, breast amputation):

5.2.1. See *5.1.1* above.

5.2.2. The patient must be known to a clinical behavioral scientist for at least six months and that clinical behavioral scientist must endorse the patient's request for genital surgical sex reassignment.

5.2.3. The patient must be evaluated at least once by a clinical behavioral scientist other than the clinical behavioral scientist specified in *5.2.2* above and that second clinical behavioral scientist must endorse the patient's request for genital sex reassignment. At least one of the clinical behavioral scientists making the recommendation for genital sex reassignment must be a doctoral level clinical behavioral scientist.

5.2.4. The patient must have been successfully living in the genetically other sex role for at least one year.

5.3. During and after services are provided:

5.3.1. The patient's right to privacy should be honored.

5.3.2. The patient must be charged only appropriate fees and these fees may be levied in advance of services.

Appendix C:
A sampling of articles on Hormone Studies

"An immunohistochemical study of the long-term effects of androgen administration on female-to-male transsexual breast; a comparison with normal female breast and male breast showing gynecomastia." Burgress, H. E.; and Shousha, S. *Journal of Pathology*, May 1993, 170 (1) pp. 37–43.

"Induction of insulin resistance by androgens and estrogens." Polderman, K. H.; Gooren, L. J.; Asscheman, H.; Bakker, A.; and Heine, R. J. *Journal of Clinical Endocrinological Metabolism*, July 1994, 79 (1) pp. 265–271.

"Testosterone administration increases adrenal response to andrenocorticotrophin." Polderman, K. H.; Gooren, L. J.; and van der Veen, E. A. *Clinical Endocrinology*, May 1994, 48, (5) pp. 595–601.

"Androgen receptor expression in the cervix of androgen-treated female-to-male transsexuals association with morphology and chain-specific keratin expression." van der Kwast, T. H.; Dommerholt, H. B.; van Vroonhoven, C. C.; and Chadha, S. *International Journal of Gynecological Pathology*, April 1994, 13 (2) pp. 133–138.

"Prolactin-producing pituitary adenoma in a male-to-female transsexual patient with protracted estrogen administration: a morphologic study." Kovacs, K.; Stefaneanu, L.; Ezzat, S.; and Smyth, H. S. *Archives of Pathological Laboratory Medicine*, May 1994, 118 (5) pp. 562–565.

"The influence of hormone treatment on psychological functioning of transsexuals." Cohen-Kettenis, P. T. and Gooren, L. J. *Journal of Psychology and Human Sexuality*, 1992, 5 (4) pp. 55–67.

"Squamous metaplasia in the penile urethra due to oestrogen therapy." Russell, G. A.; Crowley, T.; and Dalrymple, J. O. *British Journal of Urology*, March 1992, 69 (3) pp. 282–285.

Appendix D:
A sampling of articles of interest on Female-to-Male Surgery

"Late salvage of 'free flap' phalloplasty: a case report." Nordanus, R. P. and Hage, J. J. *Microsurgery*, 1993, 14 (9) pp. 599–600.

"Addressing the ideal requirements by free flap phalloplasty: some reflections on refinements of technique." Hage, J. J.; and de Graaf, F. H. *Microsurgery*, 1993, 14 (9) pp. 592–598.

"One-stage total penile reconstruction with a free sensate osteocutaneous fibula flap." Sadove, R. C.; Sengezer, M.; McRoberts, J. W.; and Wells, M. D. *Plastic Reconstructive Surgery*, December 1993, 98 (7) pp. 1314–1323.

"Phallic construction in female-to-male transsexuals using a lateral upper arm sensate free flap and a bladder mucosa graft." Hage, J. J.; de Graaf, F. H; van den Hoek, J.; and Bloem, J. J. *Annals of Plastic Surgery*, September 1993, 31 (3) pp. 275–280.

"A new design for the radical forearm free-flap phallic construction." Gottlieb, L. J.; and Levine, L. A. *Plastic Reconstructive Surgery*, August 1993, 92 (2) pp. 276–279.

"Scrotal construction by expansion of labia majora in biological female transsexuals." Sengezer, M.; and Sadove, R. C. *Annals of Plastic Surgery*, October 1993, 31 (4) pp. 372–376.

"Sculpting the Glans in phalloplasty." Hage, J. J.; de Graaf, F. H.; Bouman, F. G.; and Bloem, J. J. *Plastic Reconstructive Surgery*, July 1993, 92 (1) pp. 157–161.

"The anatomic basis of the anterior vaginal flap used for neourethra construction in female-to-male transsexuals." Hage, J. J.; Torenbeek, R.; Bouman, F. G.; and Bloem, J. J. *Plastic Reconstructive Surgery*, July 1993, 92 (1) pp. 102–108.

"Obtaining rigidity in the neophallus of female-to-male transsexuals: a review of the literature." Hage, J. J.; Bloem, J. J.; and Bouman, F. G. *Annals of Plastic Surgery*, April 1993, 30 (4) pp. 387–333.

"Preconstruction of the pars pendulans urethrae for phalloplasty in female-to-male transsexuals." Hage, J. J.; Bouman F. G.; and Bloem, J. J. *Plastic Reconstructive Surgery*, June 1993, 91 (7) pp. 1303–1307.

"Microsurgical forearm 'cricket bat-transformer' phalloplasty." Gilbert, D. A.; Jordan, G. H.; Devine, C. J. Jr.; and Winslow, B. H. *Plastic Reconstruction Surgery*, October 1992, 90 (4) pp. 711–716.

"Periurethral collagen for urinary incontinence after gender reassignment surgery." Fitzpatrick, C.; Swierzewski, S. J. 3rd; and McGuire, E. J. *Urology*, October 1993, 42 (4) pp. 458–460.

"Orgasm in the postoperative transsexual." Lief, H. I.; and Hubschman, L. *Archives of Sexual Behavior*, April 1993, 22 (2), pp. 145–155.

"Phalloplasty in female-to-male transsexuals: What do our patients ask for?" Hage, J. J.; Bout, C. A.; Bloem, J. J.; and Megens, J. A. *Annals of Plastic Surgery*, April 1993, 30 (4), pp. 323–326.

"Gender Dysphoria Syndrome." Laub, Donald R., Laub, Donald R., Jr., van Maasdam, Judy. In *Grabb Smith's Plastic Surgery, 4th Edition*, Chapter 58, pp. 1392–1404, 1991.

Appendix E:
A sampling of articles of interest on Male-to-Female Surgery

"Gender reassignment surgery for male primary transsexuals." Crichton, D. *South African Medical Journal*, May 1993, 83 (5) pp. 347–349.

"Prolapse of the sigmoid neovagina: report of three cases." Freundt, I.; Toolenaar, T. A.; Jeekel, H.; Drogendijk, A. C.; and Huikeshoven, F. J. *Obstetrics and Gynecology*, May 1994, 83 (5) pp. 876–879.

"Sex-reassignment surgery male-to-female: Review, own results and report of a new technique using the glans penis as a pseudoclitoris." Rubin, S. O. *Scandinavian Journal of Urology*, 1993, 154 pp. 1–28.

"Sculpting the neoclitoris in vaginoplasty for male-to-female transsexuals." Hage, J. J.; Karim, R. B.; Bloem, J. J.; Suliman, H. M.; and van Alphen, M. *Plastic Reconstructive Surgery*, February 1994, 93 (2) pp. 358–364.

"Comparison of two methods of vagina construction in transsexuals." van Noort, D. E.; and Nicolai, J. P. *Plastic Reconstructive Surgery*, June 1993, 91 (7) pp. 1308–1315.

"A new method for clitoroplasty in male-to-female reassignment surgery." Fang, R. H.; Chen, C. F.; and Ma, S. *Plastic Reconstructive Surgery*, April 1992, 89 (4) pp. 679–682.

"The occurrence of diversion colitis in patients with a sigmoid neovagina." Toolenaar, T. A.; Freundt, I.; Huikeshoven, F. J.; Drogendijk, A. C.; Jeekel, H.; and Chadha-Ajwani, S. *Human Pathology*, August 1993, 24 (8), pp. 846–849.

"A modified technique to create a neovagina with an isolated segment of sigmoid colon." Freundt, I.; Toolenaar, T. A.; Huikeshoven, F. J.; Drogendijk, A. C.; and Jeekel, H. *Surgical Gynecology and Obstetrics*, January 1992,174 (1) pp. 11–16.

"Construction of neovagina with preservation of the glans penis as a clitoris in male transsexuals." Eldh, J. *Plastic Reconstructive Surgery*, April 1993, 91 (5) pp. 895–900.

"Long-term psychological and psychosocial performance of patients with a sigmoid neovagina." Freundt, I.; Toolenaar, T. A.; Huikeshoven, F. J.; Jeekel, H.; and Drogendijk, A. C. *American Journal of Obstetrical Gynecology*, November, 1993, 169 (5), pp. 1210–1214.

"Gender Dysphoria Syndrome." Laub, Donald R., Laub, Donald R., Jr., Maasdam, Judy Van. In *Grabb Smith's Plastic Surgery, 4th Edition*, Part 58, pp. 1404–1409, 1991.

Bibliography

The American Psychiatric Association: *Diagnostic and Statistical Manual of Mental Disorders*, Fourth Edition, American Psychiatric Association, Washington, D.C., 1994.

Dorland's 27th Edition Illustrated Medical Dictionary, Harcourt, Brace Jovanovich, Inc., 1988.

Gilbert, David. "Transsexuals and surgery." Unpublished paper, 1995.

The Merck Manual of Diagnosis and Therapy, 16th Edition, 1992; Rahway, New Jersey.

Pfaffllin, F. "Regrets after sex reassignment surgery. Special Issue: Gender dysphoria: Interdisciplinary approaches in clinical assessment." *Journal of Psychology and Human Sexuality*, 1992 5(4) p. 69–85.

Snaith, P., Tarsh, M. J. and Reid, R. "Sex reassignment surgery. A study of 141 Dutch transsexuals." *British Journal of Psychiatry*, May 1993, 154, pp. 1–28.